PRAISE FOR *THE WORK-LIFE BALANCE MYTH* AND DAVID McNEFF

"For years I've thought that work-life balance was a myth, but I could never articulate exactly why, or suggest an alternative approach to dealing with all that was being thrown at me. Dave's Seven-Slice approach now gives voice to my feelings and thoughts. I've unknowingly been dealing with several of the Slices without fully understanding how many there were and what specific processes I should use to incorporate them into my like. Today, more than ever, Dave's insights and approaches are more timely than perhaps even he'd imagined. As we deal in the current and post–Covid-19 environment, Dave's teachings and insights will provide the guidance necessary to navigate our current and future world."

—LES BRUN, Chairman and CEO, Sarr Group

"There are many books that claim to have the answers on how to navigate the sea of competing demands in our lives. Most of them are impractical and filled with hyperbole. *The Work-Life Balance Myth* is filled with practical approaches to cope with our busy lives in ways that strengthen our relationships and make us healthier. An easy read, I highly recommend it to anyone who wants to achieve greater harmony and balance in our modern world."

—JESSE HARRIOTT, Head of Analytics, Workhuman

"Dave McNeff's Seven-Slice Method is a revelation. A user-friendly distillation of a career's worth of earned experience and wisdom into an insightful road map for behavioral change. You'll never look at how you spend your time the same way again! There are practical suggestions for how all of us—even those who think they have no time—can incorporate critical missing Slices of life into our day, and in doing so, move closer to cracking the elusive code of achieving harmony and fulfillment."

—GORDON WOODWARD, Partner and CEO, Kohlberg & Company

"You can't lead other people until you can lead yourself. You can't lead yourself until you have an understanding and a plan for how you want to live. This book is a practical guide on how to make choices and set priorities that will result in a more fulfilling and impactful life."

—TIM TOLL, CEO, Iovate Health Sciences International, Inc.

"While much has been written about work-life balance, Dave McNeff offers a refreshing and inspiring perspective that creates a path to a more fulfilling life. The Seven-Slice Method enables practitioners to avoid the two-dimensional work-life balance trap and find more meaning in every Slice of their lives."

—PATRICK SPEAR, President and CEO, GMDC/Retail Tomorrow

"Having held leadership positions for decades, I've read many books and spoken with many consultants about business leadership and management. This new book by Dave McNeff is different. Its holistic, multifaceted, real-life-centered framework sets it apart. For those of us who have had the privilege of working closely with Dave, we can now, thankfully, be joined by many more who can access his methodology through this outstanding book. A great read—and an even greater approach to life!"

—TIM OYER, President and Managing Partner, Wolf Greenfield

"For over 35 years, I have wrestled with trying to solve the work-life balance problem. This book helped me appreciate that my challenge has been focusing only on two variables of a seven-variable equation. It literally solved the problem. It has changed my life!"

—TOM SMITH, Executive Managing Director, Mason Wells Private Equity

"Dave's ability to constructively orient members of our firm to tackle their own limiting factors has enhanced the way we work together. *The Work-Life Balance Myth* provides a wider audience with tools to reframe how they can succeed across all aspects of their lives. The book substitutes the elusive goal of a work-life balance with a focus on the Seven Slices of your life and provides a road map to a more productive, impactful, and sustainable professional and personal existence."

—SAM FRIEDER, Managing Partner, Kohlberg & Company

"Dave McNeff's concept of the Seven Slices of life can help reduce daily pressure in a way that really enables readers to no longer feel locked into rigid work-life paradigms. It's a perfect book for these tension-filled times. I heartily endorse it!"

—RAKESH TONDON, Cofounder and President, Le Tote

"It is so refreshing to have finally discovered a book that puts to rest the age-old work-life balance question. The difficulty of attempting to fulfill the promise of WLB can lead to high stress. Dave McNeff offers an alternative, one in which several Slices of life replace two gigantic ones. As a result, my stress levels have already begun to decrease. Thank you, Dave!"

—KEITH COOPER, seven-time CEO and entrepreneur

"Dave McNeff's breakdown book is a great step forward. I call it a 'break-down' book because it breaks down previously common assumptions, especially that work-life balance is realistic. Instead, Dave ingeniously replaces the work-life balance myth with a new approach, the Seven Slices. This book will open your eyes to a refreshing and eminently practical work-life solution. Read it!"

—JIM HARRINGTON, VP and Chief Intellectual Property Counsel, Radius Health

"David has worked with several of my companies. I tease him by calling him a people wizard—he has a special talent in helping executives think and feel about their lives. But Dave never gives them the answers; rather, he works with people to understand their own awareness. This self-awareness helps them to be better not only at their job but in all Seven Slices of their lives."

—PETER BLACKLOW, Managing Partner, Boston Seed Capital

"Having held global senior leadership positions in both large diversified medical device companies and now a venture-backed startup, I greatly appreciate the vital role of good health and the challenges related to getting there. That is why I found *The Work-Life Balance Myth* such a breakthrough. Sound health depends on the mind and spirit. This book will enable its readers to join these two vital elements and maintain healthier lives."

—GEORGE FAZIO, President and CEO, Corvia

"The Seven-Slice Method is well worth the read. Dave's enduring message of rediscovery is one of harmony and balance."

—RUDY HAUSER, CEO, CAPInnoVet, Inc.

"Harmony and resilience. As a silk tapestry creates both through a synergy of its parts, McNeff weaves us a bespoke action plan for a harmonious life."

—BEN MAO, Partner, Kohlberg & Company

"The fundamental premise that work-life balance exists is flawed. Balance is achieved by making the Seven Slices of your life a priority. This book can help you transform your life by rethinking and reprioritizing where you place your attention."

—KATHY BOLHOUS, CEO, Charter Next Generation

"Dave McNeff points out the futility of work-life balance and offers a new framework, the Seven-Slice Method, for managing the stress in our lives. It encourages the reader to seek holistic harmony in the Seven Slices of one's life, rather than the frustrating pursuit of balance between just two, work and life. A thought-provoking, enjoyable read that offers insights into the real-life application of the method through the experiences of real people. I can't stop thinking about this book!"

—KERRY FLYNN, VP and Chief Intellectual Property Counsel, Vertex Pharmaceuticals

"Dave's book is foundational for busy executives who need to organize and prioritize their days and weeks. Recognizing and addressing the Seven Slices of life is the first step toward driving success in each of those worlds. Organizing yourself around McNeff's paradigm is a stress reliever and provides an optimal operating platform for growing businesses and their key assets—their people."

—JIM MAYNARD, Managing Director, Napatree Capital

"One could easily identify and empathize with the people and the situations described in the various case studies. We have all been there in one form or another. I thoroughly enjoyed the book's detailed diagnoses and the eventual resolutions of the individuals described in the case studies utilizing the Seven-Slice Method. A clear and concise writer, Dave McNeff does a wonderful job showing us how to understand, recognize, and incorporate the Seven Slices of life to achieve harmony and balance in one's life. I will recommend this book to my managers to read, in the hope that it will teach them how to assist their colleagues as well as themselves."

—GARY D. CHIN, President, Dauphin North America

"Dealing with stress at work often feels like having to eat an elephant. With this framework, I have seen Dave enable professionals to tackle that process, one pragmatic bite at a time. What looked like an unsurmountable challenge turned out to be (relatively) easily fixed through a fascinating process debunking the myth of work-life balance. He has written a great book here, outlining a platform for success that all executives should adopt."

—WIM SOUVERIJNS, Chief Commercial Officer, ObsEva

"Filled with wisdom and empathetic honesty. I could not stop reading this book. The way personal experiences are woven in makes it authentic. It provides insight and guidance on how to tap into all Slices of life. It enables us to see things differently and helps us live a more fulfilled existence while we are here on earth. Bravo, Mr. McNeff!"

—SUSAN A. PARKER, Senior Consultant, Waterworks

"There's no easy pill, but David gives you the easy Seven-Slice Method for unlocking the best version of yourself and your brightest future."

—PAUL A. FERREIRA, Managing Partner, Blue Hawk Investments, LLC

"McNeff has created an innovative process, addressing the compartmental-ization of our lives. These inner compartmentalizations have brought about a crisis that is reaching epic proportions, reflected in the distress of body, mind, and spirit. His effective yet simple-to-follow way of helping us toward the integration (integrity) of these divisions leads to a life of health, fulfill-ment, and hope."

—REV. DR. KEN ORTH, Healing Worship Minister,
Old South Church in Boston and Pastoral Counselor and Spiritual Director,
First Congregational Church of Winchester (MA)

"Understanding the fallacy of work-life balance proved to be a huge wake-up call. Learning the importance of touching the Seven Slices of life provided the path to gaining greater fulfillment and becoming a stronger leader."

—HARPREET GREWAL, Chief Operating Officer, Volante Technologies

"The principles laid out in Dave McNeff's book are timeless, relevant, and practical, and lead to the achievement of a harmonious and truly balanced life. There are empty spheres in our lives that we ignore and that weigh us down. Dave McNeff holds a light to these empty spheres and provides a path-way to an awareness that will positively impact not only our lives but the lives of those with whom we work and live."

—PAUL FLEMMING, Managing Principal, ESAI Power

"Trying to reconcile work and life is probably the biggest emotional stressor we have to deal with in the developed world. Beyond the two Slices that receive the most attention from us today—namely family and work—Dave's book describes how we all have to manage Seven Slices of our lives in a way that achieves harmony. His model and his examples make it easy to understand how difficult it is to perform well in one Slice in a sustainable manner, without paying sufficient attention to the other Slices as well. I found Dave's approach very relevant and very actionable."

—ALBERTO MORIANA, Vice President of Sales, Procter & Gamble Latin America

"Dave has a unique ability to get busy professionals to step back and consider a holistic approach to their lives. The Seven-Slice Method is outlined in clear terms that describe the importance of balance, even if balance is not equally weighted. Dave's narratives and case studies helped me internalize the approach and will enable readers to apply this to their own lives. This is an important read for any executive curious about professional and personal improvement."

—BRIAN POWL, Senior Pharmaceutical Marketing Executive

THE
WORK-LIFE
BALANCE
Myth

RETHINKING YOUR
OPTIMAL BALANCE
FOR SUCCESS

DAVID J. McNEFF

NEW YORK CHICAGO SAN FRANCISCO ATHENS LONDON MADRID
MEXICO CITY MILAN NEW DELHI SINGAPORE SYDNEY TORONTO

1 2 3 4 5 6 7 8 9   LCR   26 25 24 23 22 21

ISBN   978-1-260-46889-2
MHID   1-264-46889-5

e-ISBN   978-1-260-46890-8
e-MHID   1-260-46890-9

Library of Congress Cataloging-in-Publication Data

Names: McNeff, David J., author.
Title: The work-life balance myth : rethinking your optimal balance for success /
  David J. McNeff.
Description: New York : McGraw Hill, [2021] | Includes bibliographical references
  and index.
Identifiers: LCCN 2020047230 (print) | LCCN 2020047231 (ebook) | ISBN 9781260468892
  (hardback) | ISBN 9781260468908 (ebook)
Subjects: LCSH: Work-life balance. | Work and family.
Classification: LCC HD4904.25 .M396 2020 (print) | LCC HD4904.25 (ebook)
  | DDC 650.1—dc23
LC record available at https://lccn.loc.gov/2020047230
LC ebook record available at https://lccn.loc.gov/2020047231

McGraw Hill books are available at special quantity discounts to use as premiums and sales promotions or for use in corporate training programs. To contact a representative, please visit the Contact Us pages at www.mhprofessional.com.

To my sister Kathy—
she never had a chance,
so I took them for the two of us

CONTENTS

CONTENTS

Peace is a daily, a weekly, a monthly process,
gradually changing opinions, slowly eroding old barriers,
quietly building new structures.
—JOHN FITZGERALD KENNEDY

PREFACE

He stood facing the window that overlooked the parking lot and the distant horizon. Leaning forward, shaking his head, he said, "I thought this was going to be the answer."

Richard had been working for a large company on the West Coast for 18 years in a high-pressure executive position that required a great deal of travel and produced lots of stress. With two children (almost teenage and early teenage) that needed attention and love, Richard and his wife felt that his work-life balance (or rather the lack of it) was hurting the family dynamic on several levels. When his father-in-law offered Richard the opportunity to come home to Kansas City to run his investment advisory firm, he quickly accepted. He and his wife thought that moving back near family and friends and working in a comfortable family business would allow them to finally achieve a healthy work-life balance and get out from under the blanket of suffocating stress.

The first year went well for Richard and his family. They easily settled into their new home, and he learned the business while his father-in-law transitioned toward retirement.

Then year two came along and everything changed.

After Richard took over the full reins of the business and his father-in-law retired to Florida, several clients left for competing investment firms. This, of course, put instant financial pressure on the business. Richard had to let go of some longstanding employees. Sensing trouble, a few of the most talented people in the firm moved on, leaving Richard with a bigger problem. He was still learning the business, and he could not afford to have more good people exit the firm, so he borrowed money to maintain some form of order and stability in the business.

While all this was going on, his two children (ages 11 and 13) needed more attention. His eldest daughter was diagnosed with a learning disability, and his youngest daughter, who had struggled with the move to Kansas City two years ago, was having difficulty maintaining friends and was showing signs of depression. Providing both daughters with the support they needed was going to take a great deal of energy and effort from Richard and his wife.

On top of all this, Richard had lost his father a few months earlier, and now his mother, who had several serious health issues, was diagnosed with cancer and needed full-time care. She too needed more attention from Richard and his wife.

All of this, all at once. So much for achieving a work-life balance. Richard's situation now made his prior life on the West Coast seem like a walk in the park in comparison. Almost every part of his life was thrust into chaos. If things didn't stabilize quickly, the consequences could be devastating.

As the saying goes, *Welcome to my world.*

Stress and pressure impact all of us no matter our walk of life, gender, or situation. In my consulting work, I see various versions of Richard's story all the time. I work with executive teams and often engage with people like Richard who find themselves overwhelmed by unusual circumstances. And just as often, I work with people and teams suffering from a lack of effective stress management.

My role is to help people to develop their corporate executive skills and to find ways to reduce the impact of stress to become better executives and to lead more peaceful and fulfilling lives.

In this book, I share the Seven-Slice Method, a process that can help you disperse and defuse your stress so that you stay grounded even when everything seems to go wrong at once. We'll look at a number of people who have used the Seven-Slice Method to dramatically improve their stress management and to reach a more harmonious state.

The impetus for me in creating this method was the stress and pressure in my own life. It surfaced suddenly—or seemed to at the time. It seems surreal now, but more than 15 years ago my life fell into a chaotic, bubbling mess. A divorce, a business slowdown, a financial struggle, and children in college combined to throw me into an intense and unrelenting state of stress. It seemed as though every day brought new surprise problems that seemed to have no possible solutions.

This period lasted 20 months, which gave me plenty of time to figure out how I was going to find a way back to sanity. Like most people, I was quite familiar with the self-help and work-life balance messages in books and other places—but the situation was so dire, I felt I needed a permanent solution to my stress problem, once and for all. Trying to live with the stress I felt every day was not sustainable.

I started the process by seeking out and talking with experts in coping with life crises. Some of these conversations were extremely helpful, and some were quite frustrating. In particular, I felt frustrated with the people who used a standard "playbook" that sounded like a "one-size-fits-all" solution process. That was not going to help me very much.

Suddenly, something clicked in my mind, and it became clear to me. I realized that several parts of my life were all impacted during this intense period of stress, and the solution was to identify those parts and deal with them both individually and as part of a whole. All of us have Seven Slices in our lives: our Family Slice, our Professional Slice, our Personal Slice, our Physical Slice, our Intellectual Slice, our Emotional Slice, and our Spiritual Slice. These all need to be served in some fashion—and in serving them, they in turn serve us. *Meaning*, if I could recognize and fully understand all Seven Slices and put some effort and time into all of them, I would feel better and more balanced during stressful days.

The solution worked for me. And since my clients were often going through varying degrees of stress and trauma, it made sense to introduce this method to them to see if it might "take" with them, as it had with me. And so I rolled out the Seven-Slice Method 12 years ago. I held seminars a few times a year, and the results were very promising. Those clients who gave it a try all reported that it had a positive impact on their overall attitude and perspective.

As time went on, I introduced the method to executive teams as a way to get ahead of stress and pressure when they knew difficult times lay ahead. Not only did these teams find it helpful, but in fact, many told me that they had taken it home to share with their spouses and partners. All had found it to be practical and, in many cases, enlightening.

I observed that many people used the Seven-Slice Method when they encountered stressful times but would not think about it much when their stress level was more manageable. Others used the Method consistently to reduce their day-to-day stress level. With better control of their stress, some people reported to me that they found time to learn new hobbies, and a few even learned new languages. Who knew?

To be clear, the Seven-Slice Method won't make the stressful elements of your life vanish. You will always be navigating one stressful life event or another. But the Seven-Slice Method will calm you down so your ability to manage stress levels will improve very quickly. By being aware of these Seven Slices, our Slices can come to our aid and breathe calm and peace inside us during unsettling moments of terrible and seemingly hopeless and unbearable life stress.

Oh, I almost forgot. Richard embraced the Seven-Slice Method when introduced to him, in part because he was desperate for any help at that point in his life. Though the tumult of his life continued for about a year and a half, he kept himself afloat well enough to survive without stumbling, which was critical since he was the anchor that both his business and family needed during that difficult time.

Over time, and without panic, he restructured his business, and he provided his children with the extra attention and help they needed to move forward in a positive way. With treatment and assistance, his mother was able to recover and return to her healthy lifestyle.

Richard claimed this method provided a practical way to find a sense of harmony in himself so he could be there for those around him. Not quite a fairy-tale ending perhaps, but a positive end to a difficult story, for sure.

As a final suggestion, it is probably best to read this book in chunks. There is a lot to read and think about in each chapter. Thinking about the ideas and how you can apply them to your situation is what will make the most difference for you in the long run. Read a chapter, think about where you are today in each of the Seven Slices, and then start to consider where you would like to be in that Slice next week or next month. In working with people using this method, I've found that both an intellectual and emotional connection need to occur. First, we learn what it is and how to use it, and then, second, we need to believe and see the results. When this occurs, lasting and positive change in all Seven Slices of your life will happen.

The following quote from Ralph Waldo Emerson eloquently expresses what is my wish for you and all readers of this book:

"Remember that nothing can give you peace but yourself."

ACKNOWLEDGMENTS

I have always had a yearning to write. In high school, I enjoyed writing short stories and was encouraged to pursue that interest by a wonderful English teacher who was brand new to teaching at the time and whose name I cannot recall today, but I would like to thank her nevertheless, because she made a difference to me. I ended up pursuing other roads and avenues in my life but really wanted to get back to writing someday. Many people motivated and encouraged me to write this book. I wish to thank them all.

Harp Grewal was one of the original people who suggested that many people would benefit from reading about the Seven-Slice Method to help them understand how to find some relief from the steady drumbeat of stress. Thank you, Harp. We all need a catalyst! And Susan A. Parker has been a constant supporter, and her encouragement consistently helped me focus and want to finish the race as well. Her energy and enthusiasm are boundless and much appreciated.

So many friends who were quietly supportive and concerned I would like to thank and say how much the simple positive words made a difference to me. They include Wim Souverijns, who always made me feel like I could make a difference. To Brian Powl, Daren Thorborn, Filipe Rodrigues, and Chris Bartimoro, who were always happy for any good news around the progress of the book, thank you. And a special thanks goes out to Jesse Harriott for providing encouragement and intelligence from his own history as a published author. Also, to Lydie Brown and Paul de Janosi, such good friends who seemed to know how to make me laugh when it was the right time, particularly as I approached the many deadlines in this venture.

My agent, Ken Lizotte, and his wonderful team at Emerson Consulting Group, Inc. did a wonderful job of getting this project across the finish line. I am indebted to Elena Petricone for her marvelous editing skills, as well as her warm, assuring personality and style. This book needed her efforts and are much appreciated. In addition, the good work of Kevin Commins, my developmental editor, who did a superb job elevating the quality of the writing and message of the book.

And my three sisters, Kathy, Mary-Helen, and Susan, who remained steady supporters during this long process. Especially Kathy, who being disabled never had a chance to shine in life but burns bright in her own amazing way. I dedicate this book to her because she was always a motivation for me to pursue my goals because she never had a chance to pursue her own.

INTRODUCTION

For years, I have heard the same message again and again from my friends, colleagues, and clients: "My company doesn't appreciate that we need work-life balance! I can't remember the last time I *wasn't* stressed."

If you're a working professional, you've probably said the same thing at one point. And I'm sure you've encountered one of the myriad self-help books, systems, HR programs, etc., that promise you that "work-life balance" is the antidote to the stress that is keeping you up at night and negatively impacting your professional and personal relationships.

This book is intended to reset that notion and propose that there is no possibility of balance in our lives. To chase balance between your work and family is futile. Instead, I offer a new way of contextualizing your life and managing your stress: the Seven-Slice Method.

This method suggests that all our lives contain the following Seven Slices:

- The Family Slice
- The Professional Slice
- The Personal Slice
- The Physical Slice
- The Intellectual Slice
- The Emotional Slice
- The Spiritual Slice

The balancing act we are all trying to accomplish is unachievable because we are all actually living *seven* different lives, or Slices. The problem is that most of us are only pursuing two. Busy professionals who juggle countless tasks, priorities, and pressures every day are particularly prone to ceding the other five Slices of their lives (their Personal, Physical, Intellectual, Emotional, and Spiritual Slices) just to keep up with the circumstances in their Family and Professional Slices.

Some people pick up one or two other Slices through various and random methods, but many live a life focusing on the two primary Slices and leave the rest to chance. No wonder that for many people the stress of family and work feels more acute than ever: it's become their entire world. That has consequences—and it's not healthy, to say the least.

THE CONSEQUENCES OF UNMANAGED STRESS

Work-life balance may be a myth, but the problem it tries to solve—dealing with persistent stress—is very real. In fact, wanting to package this message in a book is a direct result of watching the impact that stressed-out lives have on each of us—even if we are not particularly stressed out ourselves.

As someone who's often brought in to help executive teams deal with their interpersonal issues, I can speak directly to the damaging toll that stress can have on your career and your workplace. The temptation for people (particularly for ambitious and hardworking professionals) is to grit their teeth and tell themselves to *just get through it.* In many cases, I'll have a client in charge of an executive team tell me, "Yes, everyone's stressed out, but we're adults; we'll hang in there and just get through the next quarter."

Most of the time, the client will call me shortly after to tell me that someone on the team snapped, made a terrible (and often preventable) error in judgment that financially impacted the firm, or angrily quit and/or that every meeting had dissolved into arguing and yelling.

On a company level, stressed employees are more unhappy and less productive. On an individual level, if you are unable to keep your stress from taking over your life, both your personal and professional lives will suffer.

Think back to a time in your life when you were extremely stressed (which might be right now). How did you treat the people around you? Were you able to be as patient, present, and open? Were you in the best mental place to problem-solve, analyze, and make decisions? Probably not.

This is unlikely to be a surprise to you. People can be perfectly pleasant, patient, and easy to get along with (at their job or in their household) when things are calm and easy. But when stress enters the picture, your sense of perspective shrinks. The things that are stressing you out become the center of your world. You become less patient and less available to the people you care about. You might be short or rude to your loved ones or just less present with them. You become less able to feel and express gratitude and to appreciate the good things and good people in your life. You might even start to act out of step with the values you hold dear—for instance, you might stop noticing (or caring about) the feelings of others.

THE SEVEN-SLICE METHOD— WHAT'S IN IT FOR YOU?

The Seven-Slice Method won't change your circumstances. Your life will always have stress in it—both from things you can't change and from things that you can. What I have set out to do here is provide a process and a method to identify, understand, and leverage all Seven Slices of your life. This will help you master the art and science of finding the time and patience to live (even if only briefly) in every part of your life.

Again, the problem for most professionals is that they allow two Slices, their Family and Professional Slices, to dominate their lives. The Seven-Slice Method reminds you that you have five other Slices, and each can provide you a respite and perspective—without demanding a huge time commitment.

Putting our lives in this "Slice" context can have a tremendous impact on how we feel. My hope is that the message contained in this book will open a way for you to be more in *harmony* with yourself, every day.

I've helped clients successfully implement the Seven-Slice Method for years. The wonder of this to me is that people who have decided to give this a try not only find comfort from the process but have also declared that they are happier and more satisfied. "I feel lighter" is a response I often hear from clients. They stop seeing the stressors in their life as "unfair" and rather process them as events with a beginning, middle, and end. Those "gifts" of perspective are perhaps worth the effort alone.

Moreover, more effectively managing your stress and accessing a mental state of relaxation and calm using the Seven-Slice Method won't just make you feel better; it will also benefit the people around you—the people you love, care about, and work with.

HOW TO READ THIS BOOK

Each chapter in this book will illustrate how to recognize your stress sources and to use strategies to empower you to handle all kinds of stress and pressure by living in each Slice (even if only for a few moments) every day.

In Part I, "Balance Versus Harmony," we'll dive into the myth of work-life balance, introduce the Seven Slices, explain the goal of the book, and show how you can reach a feeling of harmony.

In Part II, "The Seven-Slice Method," we'll take a deep dive into each of the Seven Slices, including the components of each Slice, signs that you may or may not be attending to each Slice in a healthy way, common issues, and ideas for how you can access an underserved Slice (especially when you don't have any time to spare).

At the end of each Slice chapter, you'll find a case study that follows people (who are fictional but based upon my real clients) who implemented the Seven-Slice Method during a particularly challenging moment in their lives. Through the ups and downs of their journey, you can glean inspiration for your own.

Part III, "Ensuring the Seven Slices Deliver Harmony," is where we put it all together. You'll learn how to tackle the Seven-Slice Method on your own and to integrate your Slices for a more consistent feeling of harmony—no matter what's going on in your life. Part Three will also offer more case studies to give you pause and inspire you.

WHO WILL GET THE MOST
OUT OF THIS BOOK?

Since much of my practice involves working with executives and professionals, the stories in this book speak most directly to what people in those positions characteristically experience. However, as I mentioned in the Preface, stress affects all of us regardless of our circumstances. Therefore, the Seven-Slice Method is there for you no matter what your professional life looks like or even if you are retired or going to school.

Something I've noticed over the years is that many of my clients, either during or after they've implemented the Seven-Slice Method, introduce the method to others. Many enjoy sharing the process with their partners, friends, and coworkers. For some, in fact, learning and practicing the Seven-Slice Method with one or more people maximizes the impact and makes them more likely to stick with it. If you're someone who benefits from working with others, you may want to consider recruiting others in your Seven-Slice journey. In addition, by sharing the ideas in this book with your partner or spouse, he or she will likely support your efforts to live more harmoniously and may even end up adopting the Seven-Slice approach, too. And you'll probably develop a better relationship as a result.

AN INVITATION TO FIND HARMONY

In this book, I invite you to rediscover yourself and once again (or for the first time) live your whole life.

Here we go.

BALANCE
VERSUS
HARMONY

Peace is a day-to-day problem, the product of a multitude
of events and judgments. Peace is not an "is," it is a "becoming."
—Hailie Selassie

Balance may be a myth, but harmony is achievable—even when you feel as though every moment of your life is scheduled and you are under constant pressure. There can never be a balance if we only allow a couple of major Slices to take up most of our time. But if we consistently invest in the other five Slices of our lives, we will manage our stress and open the door to harmony, joy, and happiness.

WORK-LIFE BALANCE
WAS ALWAYS A MYTH

One out of every four Americans is "super stressed."[1] Not just stressed, but *super stressed*. The causes include heavy workloads, family responsibilities and relationships, other relationships, and difficulties in squeezing in outside interests.[2]

The latest research indicates that stress doubles our chances of contracting heart disease,[3] exacerbates respiratory issues,[4] and can cause or worsen a host of other ailments. The sad reality is that too many of us are super stressed—to the point where it's making us sick.

This state of being super stressed often creates two instant problems: we become more unhappy, and we become less productive. Being unhappy and less productive, of course, makes us feel even more pressure—and, therefore, more stressed. It can feel like a never-ending cycle.

Anyone can handle a stressful day or a stressful week here and there. But many successful professionals live in a spiral that never seems to allow for escape. In fact, 76 percent of employees in the United States feel burned out at work, with 28 percent *always* feeling burned out.[5]

What's stressing us out? Since most people work to provide for themselves and their families, let's look at what people say is causing stress at work:

- 49 percent—low salaries
- 43 percent—lack of opportunity for advancement
- 43 percent—heavy workload

- 40 percent—unrealistic job expectations
- 39 percent—long hours[6]

Now, let's combine this with what people are feeling more broadly that is contributing to their sense of being overwhelmed. According to this same survey, here are the top seven themes that are worrying Americans today:

- 71 percent—mass shootings
- 69 percent—healthcare
- 64 percent—work
- 62 percent—current political climate
- 60 percent—money
- 60 percent—terrorism
- 56 percent—climate change[7]

To add one more log to this burning fire, consider the findings of a Cigna Insurance Company survey of over 10,000 Millennial and Gen Z workers.[8] Both groups feel lonely and isolated at work. They said there is too much texting instead of talking, which they felt promoted more detachment in relationships; too many back-to-back meetings; and very little time for ad hoc interactions with coworkers. Like everyone else, Millennials and Gen Z workers feel they are too busy and overwhelmed at the same time.

What is important to keep in mind when digesting the current state of stress from a macro level is that all these issues are impacting individuals almost every day. Very simply, most people are experiencing high levels of stress, and many people are super stressed.

COPING DEVICES

Everyone needs a way to deal with acute stress. What are some of the strategies well-meaning people choose to handle stress when it begins to become overwhelming?

In psychology, these strategies are called coping devices: they are the methods or processes people use to manage their stress. Examples of coping devices are exercise, meditation, psychotherapy, and other activities that reflect a commitment to take care of yourself. However, when everything seems to be hitting at once and people feel overwhelmed, they often feel they don't have the time to devote to their preferred coping device. Often, they turn to unhealthy coping devices, such as too much food or alcohol, substance abuse or sex, gambling, pornography, or workaholism.

A coping device allows you to stay in the Slice that is taking its toll on your mental and physical health. Sometimes it's the Family Slice, sometimes it's the Professional Slice, and often it's both. When asked, many people who utilize a coping device—healthy or unhealthy—claim the device helped them to "manage" their anxiety and stress. In essence, coping devices allow a person to blow off steam in one or more Slices of their lives.

Unfortunately, when people have an unhealthy coping device (or they take their healthy coping device too far), instead of creating "balance," the coping device actually adds to the dysfunction by introducing a new problem in the form of an addiction or obsession, which only adds to the stress and sense of "imbalance" in their life.

Please understand, this is not a criticism; it is simply another example of why we need a consistent and proven way of managing our lives away from imbalance and toward harmony.

To better understand our coping devices, we need to examine how they start.

For most of us, our coping devices begin small and with no intention on our part that they will dominate our time or energy. That is important to remember. We all tend to live in the moment; it is part of the human condition—but in the moment lies the challenge. Because in the moment lies the stress and the pain that we want to make go away. Since we don't like to remain in pain, we seek ways to numb our way through it. So we start off small with our coping devices, but over time they tend to grow, become unmanageable, and introduce new problems into our lives.

Let's take one example.

Jerry, a CFO in his mid-forties, was starting to struggle. Life had been going along pretty well. Wonderful marriage, two great kids, a nice job, and lots of assets tucked away. Then things began to unravel.

The first tangible sign of trouble was tremors in his hands. If he held on to something with a firm grip, the tremors would stop. However, right after he would let go, the shaking returned. Not only was this annoying to him; it was also getting a bit embarrassing at the office. At home, his children were starting to ask why Daddy's hands shook all the time.

As someone who was a social drinker, mostly on weekends, Jerry decided to see if a drink would help. And, of course, it did. In some ways, it was a relief. But as you can guess, there were sudden trade-offs.

Although Jerry didn't realize it at the time, the sudden hand tremors were the result of stress from a "perfect storm" of events that seemingly arrived all at once. The business that had been growing had suddenly stalled, in part due to a stress-driven decision he had made as CFO to forward future revenue into the current quarter. While the move worked in the short term, it led to a long-term problem. And when the long-term problem arrived, there was no more revenue to "pull through" from the next quarter—the stock price fell. Whenever that happens, the CFO usually gets the blame, and this was no exception. Jerry suddenly went from being a calm, confident senior leader to a nervous, worried manager of events.

At home things began to go sideways, as well. His 12-year-old son began struggling in school and was diagnosed with a challenging emotional issue. His mother-in-law developed health problems, which required his wife to leave home frequently to take care of her. Both Jerry and his wife had full plates with little time or bandwidth to support each other.

One day, Jerry revealed this to me in what was an otherwise ordinary business conversation. As he recounted what was going on in his life, I asked how he was managing it.

"OK," he answered.

After a few more questions, he admitted he was not handling it all that well. Managing the tremors through drinking was becoming a problem, particularly at home. After talking about why we all seek a coping device to self-medicate our way through high levels of stress, I offered an alternative to him.

I asked him: "What if you were able to live in Seven different Slices of your life instead of the two main ones that are causing you a terrific level of stress right now?"

He looked slightly bemused and said, "Tell me more."

I explained he had five other Slices available to him at any time of the day, all of which could help him deal with the stress he was suffering in a better and healthier way than his current strategies. He was interested.

What we found is the same thing I find with most people when we examine how many Slices they actually live in. Most of us find it hard to believe that we are not living in three or four Slices of our lives. In Jerry's case, after looking at the five Slices—the Physical, the Emotional, the Spiritual, the Intellectual, and the Personal—he determined he spent no time in the Spiritual, the Physical, and the Emotional.

When we willfully or unconsciously ignore one or more of our Slices, we often pay the price just when we need the help the most. The good news is that these Slices are always there for you, ready to be picked back up to help you get through difficult times.

THE WORK-LIFE BALANCE MYTH

Supposedly, the answer to our super stress is to achieve a better work-life balance. So many stressed professionals struggle to attain that elusive "balance" by following the advice offered in books and by various experts. You've probably attended a workshop, received an educational email from your HR department, read books, or otherwise heard about the importance of achieving work-life balance. It's become a cottage industry.

The promise is that if you try hard enough, you will achieve a mathematical balance in your life that will enable you to do all the things you need to do and want to do without the stress. Most of the suggestions in work-life literature amount to spending more time in your Family Slice and less in the Professional. But for most people, that is often not practical or effective, particularly if you're under a great deal of stress in one or both of those Slices.

Categorically, balance as typically perceived simply cannot exist—not if you must work and care for your family all the time. And this is the case for far too many business professionals; they spend almost all their time in these two endeavors. Pursuing success and happiness must necessarily take a back seat.

YOUR WORK IS NOT THE ENEMY

Many professionals blame their workplace for the lack of balance in their lives. You've probably heard many or all of these complaints: "I'm wiped out all the time because of my job," "My job is sucking the life out of me," and "It's impossible to achieve a work-life balance because my workplace asks too much of us."

While many people find it hard to grasp, the truth is, work is not the problem. As long as humans have been on the planet, we have worked in order to secure our survival. We have always had work- and family-related stress.

Of course, in the modern world of work, where people are often expected to be online and on call 18 hours a day or more, no one would deny the stakes are high. But letting stress take over your life is not the fault of work itself.

So if work isn't the enemy, what is?

The real enemy is time. Our time is limited, and everyone only has 24 hours in a day. For many people, there never seems to be enough time to do all the things they have to do and want to do.

THE PROBLEM OF ACCUMULATION

The problem of accumulation will be no stranger to those who consistently live in a state of stress. It is the situation where you find yourself dealing with too many things at once—and when the next thing happens, you're completely thrown off and discombobulated. One more difficult phone call, one more blocked roadway, or one more 6 p.m. meeting. Suddenly, you snap. Or implode.

In my experience, the event that gets you to the "snap" stage could be anything large or small. However, the challenges that had already piled up made the "next one" the final one. At that point, the accumulation of stresses caused you to simply fold or bend. It was too much for your coping abilities. Some people have described the feeling of constant stress as an "undertow" feeling—a sense that you are falling and being swept away and cannot seem to stop it.

I believe that this feeling is often a result of spending all your waking time in your Family and Professional Slices while your Personal, Physical, Intellectual, Emotional, and Spiritual Slices wither. Every issue and problem keeps piling up in those Family and Professional Slices until you cannot take one more thing.

The problem of accumulating too many problems for two Slices to handle often leads people into fear, depression, sadness, and a sinking feeling of futility. How will I ever get out of this endless downward spiral, people often ask.

Some people get to a point where they're so sick of the constant stress that they make a radical change. They quit their job, move across the country or across the world, take over their father-in-law's fly-fishing shop, sell necklaces from a hut on a beach, or make some other dramatic life-changing move.

And for some, that very well may be the best decision they ever make. But most of us, for a variety of reasons, are unable or unwilling to entirely give up the work we do and the lifestyle we enjoy.

If only we could manage our stress.

It has been my observation that more than half of the successful people I meet and work with are teetering on the edge and are only one small step from going over the edge. The way back from that edge is finding your way into the Seven Slices of your life where the accumulation problem cannot exist.

To do that, we will learn how to spend short periods of time in your other five Slices, helping to help disperse the stress and anxiety in your life. By paying attention to and spending more time in these valuable, but previously neglected, Slices of your life, you will spend less time in worry and fear. Ultimately, living this way will help stop the stress spiral.

Part of the joy in learning how to live this new way is that you gain a perspective on the size and scope of your stress. You see yourself in a different context. You become more whole and diverse rather than existing solely in a two-dimensional world of Family and Work. This begins to happen when you see that you have five other interests in your life that are there for you to access and explore for you own benefit and reward.

If work-life balance is a myth, what can we do? I argue that while we'll never be mathematically balanced in all the areas of our lives that we care about, we can better manage our stress and reach a place of harmony by recognizing and consciously living in all of our Slices.

Let's take a look at how to do this.

ATTENDING TO THE SEVEN SLICES DELIVERS HARMONY

He who lives in harmony with himself lives in harmony with the universe.
—MARCUS AURELIUS

The most common question we ask one another each day is, "How are you doing?"

From my observations working with many highly active and engaged people, their answers to that question fall into one of three categories. The first answer expresses a reasonable level of well-being and life satisfaction:

> "You know what . . . things are going pretty well, and I am doing fine!"

The second response is more targeted to the here and now:

> "I am OK, but today is going to be a little rough."

The third reveals a focus on a meaningful goal or achievement the respondent has in mind:

"Well, things are quite hectic right now, but it will be worth it in the long run, for sure."

The point of referencing these three different responses is to show that you can integrate all the above rather than be stuck in one category. Similarly, if you attend to all Seven Slices of your life, you will be able to integrate a feeling of life satisfaction while being in the here and now and looking forward to the future.

THE WORK-LIFE BALANCE MYTH AND COMPARTMENTALIZATION

By now, we all know that the Family and Professional Slices of your life take up most of the hours in your day. Yet those other five Slices of our lives that most of us neglect need time invested in them too so we can find a sense of balance and harmony in our lives every day.

In my years of working with many executives in an advisory capacity, I have noted another common challenge: many people learn how to compartmentalize their Seven Slices, or the seven areas of their lives, rather than integrating them. In essence, they learn a method where they can jump from one Slice to another—perhaps not all Seven, but more than the main two Slices. While this allows them to better cope with the demands that come from their chosen Slices, the lack of integration among all Seven Slices ends up compounding people's stress levels instead of reducing them. People choose to compartmentalize their chosen Slices because they find it works—at least for a while. In fact, many can continue it for years and sometimes decades. However, there is a consequence.

From my observation, people who compartmentalize become disconnected with themselves and the people around them. Often, lost relationships and broken marriages are the result. Compartmentalization is tempting (and sometimes addicting) because it is easy to implement and allows people to focus on things they like. But while compartmentalization can be hard to change, it is absolutely worth the effort if you want to lower your stress levels and live with a greater sense of balance and real harmony.

You have Seven Slices at your disposal to help manage your stress. By understanding and truly integrating them all, you can begin down the path toward a less stressful life.

AN OVERVIEW OF THE SEVEN SLICES

To understand how to achieve harmony, we need to understand the Seven Slices so that we can benchmark and identify what they are and how they fit into our whole life. Here is a brief overview of all Seven.

The Family Slice

This is a Slice or part of your life that is basic to all of us. Our family of origin and our own nuclear family are central to who we are.

In this Slice, you likely play several roles. You can be a child, sibling, parent, partner, and grandparent all at once, and each of these roles requires a fair amount of time and effort to do well. And because other people and your relationship to them are the focus, emotions come into play, and those emotions often trigger anxiety and stress.

Many people enjoy this Slice and run to it, particularly in times of stress in their other Slices. Others find it challenging and often attempt to avoid full responsibility. Nevertheless, for many people the Family Slice dominates much of their time, and trying to balance this Slice with other demands in their life is a big challenge.

The Professional Slice

This Slice is where you work and make your living. Along with family, it's likely the Slice that occupies the most time in your life.

The Professional Slice generates wonderful and stressful opportunities every day. In this Slice, achievement is measured on many levels, within your organization and your profession and by society. When asked about success, most people talk about their Professional Slice first. It is our natural response.

Our Professional Slice provides a wonderful challenge to grow and develop skills and talents. This Slice most often requires education, training, or on-the-job learning.

For most people, the Professional Slice is extremely important. Consequently, it impacts every other Slice in their lives.

The Personal Slice

The Personal Slice of your life is all about you and what you choose to do beyond what other people and the world see. It includes the special interests, hobbies, activities, and personal pursuits that matter to you and only you.

The Personal Slice is an important part of life—but people often neglect it. A term we hear a lot these days is "self-care," and however you think about self-care, it is a process primarily located in your Personal Slice. What goes on in the Personal Slice is what aids and comforts you as you live your life.

The Physical Slice

You only have one body, and how you take care of it matters. Many people tend to take their bodies for granted. While they may wish to exercise regularly and eat a healthier diet, for many busy people a crowded schedule and competing priorities will make this difficult to do so consistently.

Physical fitness helps us to feel better, not only physically, but mentally, and it helps us to avoid chronic health problems that surface when we carry too much weight and are out of shape. Paying attention to your body and maintaining healthy habits can help you look younger, improve your quality of life, and keep your immune system strong to fight off illnesses.

When your body is in good physical shape, it makes the rest of your life easier. When your health is suffering, everything else just gets harder to handle because you have pain to deal with, and that negatively impacts your other Slices.

The Intellectual Slice

This Slice is where your intellectual curiosity lives. And what is curiosity? Fundamentally, it is the desire or interest to learn something new. This Slice reflects the things you think about and specifically what you want to learn or relearn. To identify your interests in this regard, ask yourself what you like to read just to learn or enjoy.

It's important to understand that achievement is not required for this Slice. No one is measuring or judging you here. It is about the decisions you make (or don't make) to keep yourself stimulated and engaged in your life.

The Intellectual Slice is a special part of our lives, and it's one you might want to think about for some time, particularly if you've been ignoring it.

The Emotional Slice

This Slice of your life focuses on you and how you think and feel about yourself and about the events and circumstances of your life. The Emotional Slice is the area where we experience emotions as we go through any situation or circumstance. It's also where our bodies and behaviors react to the emotions we feel. Even though it may seem like we spend little to no actual time in this Slice, we experience emotions every day as we simply go about living our daily lives.

Now, I know many people will push back here and say, "I'm not an emotional person," but the reality is we all experience emotions, and we all make decisions in how we deal with our emotions. We all know people who seem walled off from their feelings, but that doesn't have to be your reality anymore. Over many years of working with many people, I've discovered that whenever we put off dealing with a painful or uncomfortable feeling, it always resurfaces in some form later in our lives, and often becomes even more painful and difficult to process.

The Spiritual Slice

This is the area of your life that is not seen, but you believe is real. The Spiritual Slice is where our faith, values, beliefs, and philosophies are nurtured and developed. For most of us, it is a calming place to be.

Note that the Spiritual Slice doesn't mean you should pursue a religion—rather, it's in this Slice where you ask yourself: "What do I believe? What are my fundamental values and why? Am I living in accordance with them?"

Regardless of our religious beliefs, we are all yearning for that larger context that can put our day-to-day lives in a perspective that is comforting and revealing.

THE HAPPINESS CAVEAT

Of course, there's a difference between "not stressed" and "happy." In behavioral science, happiness ultimately is a decision. We know there are people in the exact same circumstance, and one person will find happiness and the other won't. Being "out of stress" doesn't necessarily mean you'll be happy, but it gives you a better shot at it.

The happiness the Seven-Slice Method offers is slightly different than how most people think of happiness. Our process requires you to take an inventory of your life and work to control the things you can control so that you feel more harmonious within yourself and with the world.

There's a ripple effect as you do this work. As your awareness grows and the facets of your life come into view, you will develop the sense that you're pursuing a deeper purpose that reflects your true identity. Over time, your life will seem more meaningful and worthwhile.

In reality, it is hard to be fully happy in every area of your life all the time. But by committing to live in all Seven Slices of your life, you will get a practical perspective on Slices where you are happy and Slices that still need more positive attention. While there is plenty of happiness that you can pursue in all Seven Slices, it's unlikely you will find total happiness in all Seven at the same time.

If behavioral scientists are right and happiness is a decision, the question becomes, "What goes into that decision, and what are the criteria?" As I describe in this book, I believe that the decision on whether you are happy or not should include an assessment of all your Slices, not just one or two. And while attending to all Seven Slices won't guarantee happiness, it will help you to better define what makes you happy, as well as help you to manage your stress levels and give you the space to pursue things that really matter to you.

GOOD HARMONY

We are living in a time where there are lots of things that keep us on edge and disconnected. Being interconnected is the opposite of being disconnected, of course. Being interconnected starts with you. This Seven-Slice Method encompasses every facet of your life and provides a means to develop a deeper connection with yourself and with those around you.

When people feel interconnected or integrated with themselves, they often describe themselves as feeling "good." They usual mean that they have a deeper sense of being fully whole so the entirety of their life feels good. In Hebrew, the word used for good is "tov." It suggests that the feeling of good is connected to the overall good in your life.

These days, the world does not seem to be in any kind of harmony. But as individuals, we can achieve a feeling of harmony, tov, or good by discovering a more whole way to live in ourselves and in this world. We cannot change the world, certainly, but we can change the way we think of ourselves and how many parts of ourselves are fully alive in us and in the world. Then we can bring this good feeling and the sense of being connected in ourselves to others. As a result, we'll feel more at peace with ourselves, and we'll feel a new level of happiness.

To access harmony consistently, you don't need to make the Seven-Slice Method habitual, but you'll probably have to come close. Once you find your rhythm in accessing your Slices, harmony starts to happen. But if you pick up the Method for a few days and then put it down for a while, it won't work that well. However, if you say, "I'm going to do something every Tuesday from 5:00 to 5:30 p.m.," you start to depend on it, look forward to it, and gain a sense of harmony.

Harmony means that you smile more. Harmony means that you bring a brighter attitude to each day despite whatever work or stress you face. Harmony means that you don't lose your mind at an unexpected traffic jam. Harmony means you feel "lighter" even when the circumstances in your life are heavy. When you have a sense of harmony, your daily life feels more manageable, and you enjoy it more. The big problems suddenly appear in a different context, and solutions seem more readily available. The world seems less dark.

Let's return to the question that opened this chapter: "How are you doing?" The hope is that by utilizing the Seven-Slice Method, when you say "Good," that you really are, and that you feel more in harmony with yourself and with the world.

THE SEVEN-SLICE METHOD

The life of inner peace, being harmonious and without stress,
is the easiest type of existence.
—Norman Vincent Peale

I n Part II, we'll learn more about each of your Seven Slices, or areas of your life: the Family Slice, the Professional Slice, the Personal Slice, the Physical Slice, the Intellectual Slice, the Emotional Slice, and the Spiritual Slice. We start with the Family Slice because the Family Slice influences how you view all your other Slices.

A caveat before we begin. The Seven Slices are our whole lives put in one particular context. Maybe for some of us, for the first time. There are people who live naturally in all Seven Slices but are simply unaware of it on a formal basis. They say, after going through each Slice, "Oh, I do that," but they make up a small percentage of the population. In fact, when people first embark on this process, the two most common remarks that I hear are "Wow, it's amazing! I didn't know I spent *zero* time in three Slices of my life" and "I spend quite a bit of time in these other Slices—but I'd never realized it."

The goal of Part Two is to raise awareness that we all have Seven Slices that we need to bring front and center in our minds and lives. Each day, you have these Seven Slices that are part of you and that you can spend time in. What happens to most people is over time our priorities take over and our time goes to where it's "needed" the most. For most of us, our work and family dominate our priority list.

It makes sense that most of our stress comes from our Family and Professional Slices—after all, that's where we typically spend most of our time. When many people reach that realization, they feel a bit deflated: "I see that most of the stress in my life comes from those two Slices, and I spend most of my time there. How am I ever going to get out of stress?"

The Seven-Slice Method shows you how to manage your stress by using your other five Slices to gain a perspective on how you're choosing to live. The other five Slices, or areas of your life, are also just as available as your Family and Professional Slices. They are there to help you live a whole life, which is how you can disperse and manage the stress that comes out of the dominating two. Your Seven Slices can be taken on one at a time, or they can be combined and tackled simultaneously. As you read Part Two, ask yourself:

- "What Slices am I spending very little time in?"
- "What Slices am I spending a lot of time in, and should I be a little more cognizant about it so I can get even more out of them?"
- "How can I learn to spend time in underserved Slices, and how do I build a discipline to do it?"

At the end of each chapter, you'll follow a "character" putting the Seven-Slice Method to work at a particularly stressful moment in that person's life. The characters you will read about are real-life examples that have been fictionalized for the purpose of this book. They are based upon the clients I've worked with over many years who utilized the Seven-Slice Method to gain a greater sense of calm and control amid their successful, busy lives.

You'll notice that in all the stories, or case studies, the characters don't just face one challenge, or one stressor. Rather, their stories begin at a moment when everything in their life seems to be going wrong. Their work life is faltering, their home life is tense, and maybe they've just received a notice that they're being audited by the IRS.

That's intentional—you've probably experienced an "everything-at-once" overwhelm at least once in your life. We all live complicated lives. Part Two will help you manage your stress and circumstances with conscious deliberation rather than living in a state of reaction. Furthermore, you'll also notice that no two people engage with the Seven-Slice Method in the same way. Rather, people evaluate their Slices, take stock of their own preferences and limitations, and work with what they have.

Once you understand and appreciate all your Seven Slices, you stop seeing life as being fair or unfair. Life becomes something you manage and work through rather than something where you feel victimized or overwhelmed.

The good news is that you can touch one or more of your other Slices in minutes, not necessarily hours. The important thing is to be consistent and intentional in your practice. You'll struggle to reap the benefits of the Seven-Slice Method if you only approach your Slices randomly.

The process is just a process, and you can apply it as it fits into your life, your personality, your own expectations, and your style. You'll learn from the stories that you can apply the method to best fit you and your circumstances. That's the beauty of it.

The Seven-Slice Method works because we all have these Seven parts inside us. All this process does is to bring to the surface the dormant parts of our life that we can tap into to reduce our stress and achieve greater fulfillment. It has worked for many of my clients. I am confident it can work for you.

THE FAMILY SLICE

The Family Slice isn't just big—it's huge. In this Slice, you play several roles. As mentioned earlier in the book, you can be a child, sibling, parent, partner, and grandparent all at once, and each role requires a fair amount of time to do well. Whatever the current shape of your family or what your family history may be, your Family Slice is likely to be one of your dominating Slices.

Moreover, the basis for how we manage transitions—or the passage from one state, stage, subject, or place to another—begins with our experience of transitioning within our own families. In the first 15 to 16 years of your life, you adopted habits and behaviors that played a major role in how you navigated adulthood, including how you handle stress.[1] In the Family Slice, you unknowingly (and sometimes unwillingly) learned countless skills that you needed later in life to function at your best level.

TWO AREAS OF HUMAN DEVELOPMENT— AND WHY THEY MATTER

If you've ever wondered why you handle pressure and stress the way you do, the answer is likely found in the environment you grew up in. Every family environment is unique and establishes norms and codes of conduct. The way you identify and react to difficult things, your work ethic, your morals, your priorities, and your aspirations—all are likely rooted in the environment you grew up in. Even if you stopped speaking to your family the moment you turned 18, your formative years are likely still influencing your behavior today—both at work and in the family you've established as an adult.

To better understand your tendencies and behaviors in stressful times, let's look at two areas of human development: trust and socialization.

First Area of Development: Trust

Trust can have many meanings. For our purpose in discussing human development, we're concerned with what *Merriam-Webster's Dictionary* describes as an "assured reliance on the character, ability, strength, or truth of someone or something" and "one in which confidence is placed."[2]

This may be a difficult notion to accept, but the level of trust we hold in adulthood develops when we're babies. The famed psychologist Erik Erikson claimed babies start developing trust from birth and the process continues until they are about 18 months old.[3] A baby who builds a healthy level of trust feels, "I am safe. I'm not at risk." Once you reach 18 months, your level of trust (or lack of it) is more or less set, although certainly other experiences later in life may impact your baseline trust level.

The point is, we all have a level of trust today, and it came from somewhere and from someone (or several "someones") in our past. From today's perspective, we can only look back at the people in our family that provided trust and determine if the trust level we developed from them served us well as we matured into adults.

As you observe your current family today, it's important to consider how well you're fostering trust with those around you. As a parent, the trust your children develop starts with you. When you look at yourself and embark on the Seven-Slice Method, you should answer these three questions: "Based on your childhood, how much trust do you have in the world around you?," "How does that manifest in your daily interactions?," and "How might that manifest when you're stressed out?"

If you had a healthy experience in trust building as a baby, you likely developed a reasonable amount of confidence and self-esteem. If so, it's a wonderful gift that originated from your Family Slice.

Confidence and self-esteem are sometimes confused with each other. Though many people tend to conjoin them, it's important to remember that confidence and self-esteem are two different things. Confidence is a result of practicing something enough times that you know you can do it. Self-esteem, on the other hand, is what you think and feel about yourself as a person. Ask yourself: "What kind of friend am I?" And/or "What kind of spouse, parent, sibling am I?" The answers likely reflect your level of self-esteem.

I often observe my clients conflating the two. They rise and fall emotionally based on their perceived performance in each Slice of their lives. They live on a roller coaster of emotions, which then impacts behaviors in every facet of their lives.

The example that speaks most directly to this comes from the Professional Slice. If my confidence and self-esteem are tied together, my job performance controls the two as if they were one. Therefore, when the project that I am leading stumbles or fails, I am crushed on every level. The feeling of failing permeates my life because I believe I am only as good a person as my job performance dictates.

However, when my self-esteem and confidence are properly accounted for in my Emotional Slice, I can look at the job performance as just that, my job performance, rather than *the* event that defines my self-worth. When I'm aware that what I do is separate from who I am, then the roller coaster effect tends to disappear entirely. Disappointing performance does not take away from who I am and my ability to be a good person, friend, partner, and/or parent.

Some are lucky enough to have been raised to recognize this distinction, and they avoid torturing themselves when they make a mistake. There's no going back, of course, but the good news is that if you didn't enter adulthood with healthy self-esteem, it's never too late to learn it.

Second Area of Development: Socialization

Our socialization skills—meaning how we interact with others and how we behave in socially acceptable ways—are also formed in our Family Slice. Our early life finds each one of us tethered to "the mother ship," the family, and we take what we learn there when we are introduced to people and society. Our parents and caretakers usher us into the world, and the social norms of the culture are embedded in us right away.

In addition, we learn firsthand the rules of engagement, and we often mimic the behaviors we see at an early age. Research seems to indicate that young babies and children learn languages easily because they watch and listen so intensely to adults speak and retain the sounds and remember and then connect the sounds to the messages sent by the adults.[4, 5] (Too bad we don't retain that innate skill into adulthood!) We also learn by observing how

25

our siblings (and other family members close in age) behave inside and outside the family environment.

Our next level of socialization comes from our peer group. We're introduced to peer groups through informal play dates and gatherings, and eventually through school, which is where we learn the "rules" of socializing in an organized environment. We learn to say please and thank you, to respect each other, to let our friends finish speaking before we speak, and so on.

Friendships are critical because we're communal beings. Our ability to make and maintain friendships is a real-life skill. Some of us are good at it, and some are not. In any case, how you approach and maintain friendships is likely influenced by your Family Slice.

From childhood to adolescence to young adulthood, it is quite a journey, and the learnings stay with us for the rest of our lives. But the point is, much of what we learned originated at some level in our Family Slice. It was there that we shared our day and were supported if needed and cheered if possible. This amazing Slice of our life is where we returned every day for most of our first two decades. Nothing that happened during those important formative years was a waste of time or purpose. We retain the memory of our young lives forever.

Something I have always marveled at is how people retain their early memories so vividly as they live out into their seventies and eighties. As they think back, though they could not remember what they had for lunch yesterday, they clearly remember their friends they rode the swing with and chased around the playground as children.

In today's world, social media plays a part in how young people are socialized to the world, although the degree of influence varies considerably from person to person and how and where they spend their time online.

A family's spiritual life and religious practices also play a role in the social development of children. Every religion and spiritual belief system has its own rituals, ceremonies, and holidays. These customs, habits, and beliefs contribute to people's awareness of themselves, others who share the same beliefs, and those who have differing beliefs. Even when not practicing our faith on a regular basis, we all seem to pause and reflect during the great holidays of the year. As we grow into adulthood, we tend to adopt some or all of these rituals as we start our own families—and so the cycle continues.

The final socializing experience in the Family Slice is work. Many years ago, most children were encouraged by their families to work at part-time jobs and/or summer jobs during the school break. While many young adults still earn their first paychecks in high school, the notion of "work" outside of school has widened to include a myriad of camps and volunteering opportunities. Whatever the setting, work contributes a great deal to our social development while in the Family Slice as a young person.

From a family perspective, meeting and working with people that are not family, friends, or schoolmates is a change and an entry point into another level of social development. Work is unique because we learn so much there that is different from every other Slice of our lives. It's unique because we are now reporting to someone other than family members or school authorities. Moreover, we receive a financial reward that is contingent on following instructions.

Going to work and doing your job teaches two important things: independence and problem solving. Independence comes in the form of spending time outside of the home and school; it's spending time where your performance is measured and rewarded with a monetary component. For the most part, this is our first experience receiving value for our own work, and as such, it introduces a new form of recognition. For some of us, this is an exciting moment, and it can trigger new motivations and interests. For instance, working as a social media assistant for a nonprofit may help someone discover a love for marketing and set the person on a long-term career path. For others, their first jobs are simply an interesting means to an end: "I will get a job so I can buy that used car."

Many children learn that it is rewarding to be recognized by new adults who supervise and reward their individual efforts. It is different from home recognition, recognition at school, or sports recognition. And it is typically an independent experience. Family members, classmates, and friends are likely not there for support. It is a fantastic platform where young people can grow and develop and still be able to go home to the family for support but without needing the family's protection or oversight.

Young people typically learn a great deal about problem solving on their first jobs, and those experiences can stay with them for the rest of their lives. Almost always, young people are doing things for the first time in their first jobs. Every day can bring something new to learn. Whether the first job is in retail, hospitality, or landscaping, there are rules to follow and new instructions related to the job. A teenager employed at a restaurant might be told to empty the dishwasher, stack the plates, and bring out the pot of soup simmering on the stove. What? In some cases, that kid may never have emptied his own family's dishwasher at home, and yet here that is the order of the day.

That, and "Get going!" Learning how to figure out the tasks involved in first jobs builds a natural sense of pride and contributes to a sense of self-worth and confidence. Having learned the tasks involved in that first job, the young person gets to happily say, "I've got this."

And all the while, you get to go home and report to your family the things you learned, knowing that it is a safe place and people will support and encourage you to continue to venture into society to gain more valuable experiences. A lot happens in the Family Slice, and it impacts us through our entire lives in countless ways—both good and bad. It's worth it to revisit your Family Slice to understand how it affects you physically, emotionally, and intellectually.

FRIENDSHIPS AND FOUND FAMILIES

Friendships also have a strong influence over how you socialize with others and interact with the world. They are particularly relevant for people who, for whatever reason, don't connect with their family of origin.

In many cases, your "found family" might influence your development just as much as or even more than your birth family. Your found family could include friends, teachers, youth pastors, and other mentors who supported you at important times of your life. The bottom line is that throughout your childhood and young adulthood, you're taking cues and absorbing norms from the people around you.

LOVE: THE BEST AND MOST COMPLICATED ASPECT OF THE FAMILY SLICE

While all Slices are important, your Family Slice created your first environment and established the norms for interacting with and reacting to the world around you. As a result, it is often the Slice where it is most difficult to manage stress and pressure as an adult.

This is the only Slice of your life where the glue is love—whether that love is pure, impure, healthy, or unhealthy—between you and other people.

This is a stark difference from the Professional Slice, where the goal in your relationships with other people is likability or cooperation.

Love—in all its forms—makes the stakes in the Family Slice especially high and the stress especially difficult to navigate. Each decision you make in the Family Slice—including decisions about raising children, marrying or partnering, and divorcing, as well as how you provide financially for your family and how you support aging relatives who need extra assistance—contains extra layers of complication due to the factor of love and what expectations you, your family, and your culture might bring to it. Moreover, it's rare for people to juggle only one tension or challenge in their Family Slice—usually there are multiple things going on.

CHECKING IN WITH THE STRESS LEVEL IN YOUR FAMILY SLICE

For some people, it's obvious when their family-related stress is out of control. But for successful professionals who are used to buckling down and telling themselves, "It's fine. I'll just get through it," identifying when their Family Slice stress is spilling over might be more difficult.

Signs Your Family Slice Is Suffering

Here are some signs that you have an unhealthy relationship with the stress in your Family Slice:

- **You don't want to go home.** At the end of a long workday, you don't feel good about returning to your family. You might go home anyway, be responsible, and take care of your duties, but you're not excited about it. Alternatively, you might find reasons to not go home when you should.

- **Mental and emotional fatigue.** The feeling of being run down can manifest at work by being disengaged, struggling with concentration, or becoming less productive—even though you really love or are generally satisfied by your work.

  Your coworkers may notice this before you do. If you're being asked questions like, "Hey, is everything OK? You don't seem yourself lately," that could signal that your Family Slice stress is bleeding into your other Slices.

- **You can't stop talking or thinking about your family-related issues.** This is most obvious when someone at work or elsewhere asks how you are, and you just can't stop yourself from oversharing all the things that are stressing you out.

  By oversharing I don't mean giving the people you interact with a heads-up about your emotional state, such as, "Hey, just so everyone knows, my partner is due to go into labor any day now, so I might be checking my phone more often." By oversharing, I mean you go on at length about personal details with people you barely know. "My daughter stole my car. What am I going to do?" you say when you are checking out at the grocery store. "I don't know, sir. I'm just the cashier."

  I've had to deal with this a lot in my career in working with clients. When the stress in the family exceeds someone's acceptable level and the person starts to display it in the professional workplace, it makes everyone uncomfortable.

  In the Professional Slice there is no room for family. Even when you need help in your Family Slice, you cannot bring too much of it to the workplace.

  Two other reasons why oversharing at work is a problem. Reason one, what often happens is that your coworkers (even if they're uncomfortable) will want to help and offer advice. It's a generous impulse, and sometimes it can be helpful, but it often amounts to going down a rabbit hole where your coworkers are providing counseling without a license. Reason two, you may not be aware of it, but you could very well be harming your professional relationships, and that could have real consequences. "I can't talk with Steven anymore; he won't stop complaining about his wife," a colleague might say to your boss. Or a superior might think, "I thought Susan was up to the task, but maybe she can't handle this work after all."

An inability to stop thinking about the stress in your Family Slice might also manifest in less obvious ways, such as difficulty in being present with people who are important to you.

Bottom line: when you find yourself constantly thinking or talking about your marriage woes, problems with the children, problems with your parents, your struggles trying to make the Family Slice work—that's the signal you need help in that Slice; and you really can't lean on your Professional Slice for support. Instead, you should look to your other five Slices for a lifeline.

Signs Your Family Slice Is in Good Shape

Here are some signs that you've got a healthy relationship with your Family Slice:

- **You look forward to going home.** Granted, there are times when your family life will be stressful no matter what (for instance, when you have a new baby), but generally you are happy to return home and be with your family.

- **You're present and available to the people who are important to you, even when you're under stress.** You can set aside whatever stressors are going on and really pay attention to another person, whether it's your spouse, your child, or your friend. In other words, you're not just physically in the room or on a call with someone—you're also available for conversation and feedback.

- **You're patient even in the face of extra requests.** Everyone you have a relationship with will make extra requests of you from time to time. "Can you pick up dinner?" "Can you read me a story?" "Can you help me with my résumé?" "Can you help me with my lawn mower?"

  When you're managing your stress well in your Family Slice, these requests won't anger or upset you. Even when you do have to turn some requests down, you do so with patience.

Your Family Slice is in good shape when you're able to manage your stress and not let it dominate your thinking. If this sounds like you, then it's likely you've unconsciously already put the Seven-Slice Method to work.

DISCERNING BETWEEN A SYMPTOM AND A PROBLEM

A skill that can serve you well in your Family Slice (and other Slices) is the ability to discern the difference between a symptom and a problem. We want to solve problems, not symptoms. Many people don't know the difference.

For instance, say you're constantly late for dinner at home with your family, and it's becoming a point of tension between you and your spouse. You're stressed out every night you can't get home on time because you know it will lead to a fight.

Being late for dinner, however, isn't a problem—rather, it's a symptom. It's the *why* you're late for dinner that's the problem, and the problem is where you want to focus your attention for finding a solution.

If you're always late for dinner because you constantly underestimate the severity of the rush-hour traffic, the problem is direct and the solution easy: you can push your family dinners back to a more realistic time, and then you won't be late.

But maybe you claim that you're always late for dinner because "I just need to finish up a few things at work." Ask yourself what's going on there: Is your boss being unreasonable? Are you not managing your time during the day very well? Or would you rather be at work or elsewhere than with your family?

Sometimes accurately identifying the problem means facing something you would rather avoid. But until you start to solve for the true problem, you're just going to be perpetuating a symptom.

Think about the list of stressors in your life. Can you differentiate between the symptoms and the true problems? It has been my experience with clients that when they list and examine their symptoms, the problems seem to just appear. In other words, they become visible. For a lot of people, I have found that while there are many symptoms, they lead to one problem: *they simply don't want to do it.* For example, the problem might be, "I never return your phone calls, but I always have an excuse." But when the person examines the excuses, it all leads back to one problem: "I don't want to return your calls." Which leads to the realization that "I need to get my arms around why I don't want to return the calls." Once the person figures that out, then the problem gets resolved one way or the other. As opposed to continually chasing symptoms, which might manifest as, "Oh I promise I'll call you tomorrow"—and of course tomorrow never comes.

SLICE CASE STUDY: GWEN

Gwen was a seasoned pharmaceutical executive who had done well for 20 years and had never broken through to the senior or vice president level— until now.

Gwen was tasked to run a department that had just burned through two prior leaders who could not handle the situation. The department had historically been held in low esteem, but the current CEO wanted the department to become a central focus for the company's new strategy. This meant that not only would the new leader of the department have to be an expert on work process, but in addition the person would have to excel in communicating across the company to achieve buy-in for the CEO's strategy. Upper management was not thrilled with Gwen's appointment (her two predecessors were men), but due to the CEO's interest level, failure was not an option. I was brought in to give Gwen the support she would need in her new role.

Gwen was a quick study and a self-made executive, meaning she had never asked for nor received any assistance along the way. According to the reviews that she shared with me, she was a tough but fair boss—but also one who could occasionally "steamroll" people who disagreed with her approach and decision-making.

Gwen's communication ability was the number one concern. She had a slight German accent when she spoke English, and when she spoke quickly, listeners sometimes missed words if she did not pause. This was a concern because the role required Gwen to make presentations to various cross-functions within the company and occasionally to the board of directors to update progress and results.

When we first met, it was clear that Gwen was an extrovert and was brimming with confidence. Her thinking style was clearly based on facts and process, but she understood that people mattered on business teams.

One of her most noticeable traits was her level of intensity. She was driven to succeed in every aspect of life. Whether she was putting a business plan together or hosting a dinner party for 12, she had to do her best or not do it at all.

In my experience, I have noticed that people with this approach to life tend to experience a great deal of highs and lows and struggle to keep an even keel. They are exuberant when things go well but suffer great bouts of sadness when things go poorly.

People with this level of drive can be exciting and productive, but they are at greater risk of burning themselves out, as well as the people around them.

To her credit, Gwen was open to learning how she could improve her job performance, and she was comfortable in taking constructive suggestions on areas of improvement.

As you might imagine, with this sort of profile she had many strong supporters and many great detractors. With this as a backdrop, Gwen and I sat down to work on her issues and prepare her to succeed in her new role.

Gwen started very well. In the first year in the role, she grew the Shared Services division of the company from 4 to 24 people. Her first-year review was very good and contained less criticism than her previous reviews.

We built a good working relationship, and she, being a very structured person, always came to our meetings prepared and with a written agenda of items to discuss and resolve. To this point, she would set an agenda for a meeting about once a quarter where the agenda was "just fun topics." Even fun was scheduled!

At about the year and a half mark in the new position, Gwen hit a bump in the road. Her team was doing well, but there was feedback that her behavior had backslid somewhat into the rough and tumble style from her past. However, at the same time she was also quite confident, and her department was succeeding in the organization.

The human resources partner assigned to her department tried giving her feedback regarding her behavior, but Gwen was hearing none of that. She defended herself by pointing to the record of success and the fact that she was the first person in this role to achieve what the CEO had envisioned for years.

Sometimes we can be our own worst enemies, and I was beginning to sense that we were approaching that road sign on the highway.

At this point, and for reasons unrelated to job issues, stress became a problem for Gwen. And as is often the case, her outside stress began to impact her Professional Slice.

Gwen, who could be very charming when relaxed and at ease, became guarded when under stress. She did not have to say anything verbally; her nonverbal body language said it all. Her primary "tell" was her facial expressions and tone of voice. It was as though she were walking under a dark cloud. When this occurred, her team members would tiptoe around her. They avoided giving her difficult news and disengaged from her as much as possible.

That was a problem, of course, because every leader needs to hear pertinent information—good or bad. And when a team gets reticent to engage, the leadership effectiveness begins to plummet. And so it began.

To her credit, Gwen reached out to me at this point and asked if we could meet weeks before our next scheduled monthly session. When we met, I found a quite different Gwen sitting in her office.

Her voice said it all as she smiled and said, "Hello."

I have always told my clients who are in leadership and management positions, every relationship gets built every day at "Hello." When we get it right, the relationship seems to grow day by day, and when we get "Hello" wrong every day, the relationship seems to diminish and grow dim. At our "Hello," it was clear to me that Gwen's relationships were suffering.

Gwen was ready to open up about the stress she had been bringing into the office. She was fresh out of a meeting with her direct supervisor, who made it clear that though her team was performing well, the team morale was suffering and her peers were complaining about her near bullying behavior in group meetings. She was clearly shaken by this feedback. She had a tough time maintaining eye contact with me, which sometimes indicates that the "fight-or-flight" response has been triggered.[6]

She explained that there were things going on in her life that were causing tremendous angst for her. Gwen shared that she recently received test results regarding a potential heart ailment. She was told that if she didn't change something in her lifestyle, she could potentially develop a more serious heart condition. The diagnosis had rattled her since her health had always been excellent. At the same time, her family and personal life were generating tremendous challenges that required her attention and energy.

In her Family Slice, her mother in Germany who lived alone and was estranged from Gwen's brother was not physically well and needed help. Although Gwen was never close with her mother and always believed that she was never quite good enough in her mother's eyes, she felt she needed to travel to Germany shortly to deal with that situation at a time when she was struggling with her role in the company. In addition, Gwen had a fractured relationship with her ex-husband, and co-parenting her daughter who was a senior in high school had become a bit of a nightmare for her. Further, while she had been in a committed relationship with her boyfriend for years, she was now questioning whether she should continue since she found herself losing interest in him over the past several months.

"Well," I asked, "is there anything else?"

It was the first time she laughed during our meeting. Of course, it's hard to laugh when you feel like you are in an undertow of problems. I suggested that her current situation truly qualified as a full plate of life problems, and there was no wonder she was struggling—anyone would be.

I asked her why she thought she had waited this long to talk with someone about her challenges. Her answer was common among successful people. People come to *her* for help, she explained. "The helper," "the fixer"—those were roles that she knew how to play. Seeking help for herself? That was new territory for her.

Gwen then explained that because she felt so overwhelmed, it had become difficult to concentrate and focus on one thing at a time. Moreover, all Gwen seemed to notice anymore in her team members was how wrong they seemed to be and how many mistakes they were making. When meeting with groups, she would single people out and tear into them publicly. At this point, she saw how her behavior had damaged morale.

Now that she could see the problem, I asked if solving or fixing it was possible. She paused before answering and then said: "That is a hard one to answer, honestly. I know I'm right. But they just seem to want to disagree—even though later, they admit I was right most of the time."

At that point I asked Gwen a simple question: "If you had to make a choice, would you rather be happy or right?"

She paused and explained in a great deal of detail why she, in order to be happy, would have to be right. Basically, her indomitable self-starter style since she was a child had served her well. She was smart, ambitious, and competitive and had led a very productive life. And she stated that she was convinced that those qualities would get her through this next "rough patch" just fine, if she could just get the energy and confidence to move forward. She felt immobilized with fatigue and fear as she stared at all she had in front of her. She wondered how she could possibly get through it all.

Gwen's Seven-Slice Plan

As we began to walk through each challenge, I decided it would be easier for Gwen to understand the source of her problems through the prism of the Seven-Slice Method.

After she took a few swings at the pie chart (see Chapter 10 for more) and assessed the percentage of time she spent in all Seven Slices, she came up with this profile of her life:

- The Family Slice: 15 percent
- The Professional Slice: 75 percent
- The Personal Slice: 5 percent
- The Physical Slice: 0 percent
- The Intellectual Slice: 3 percent
- The Emotional Slice: 1 percent
- The Spiritual Slice: 1 percent

As with most people who look at how they allocate the time in their lives for the first time, Gwen was surprised by the imbalance. To help her dig deeper into the root causes and help her strategize, I posed the following questions regarding her dormant Slices:

The Personal Slice

- What did you used to enjoy about spending time pursuing your personal interests?
- When and why did you stop spending time in this area of your life?
- What would you like to do in this area if you had to do something today?
- Is there an activity you used to do you would like to get back to?
- Is there a new interest you have always wanted to pursue that might capture your interest today?

The Physical Slice

- How happy are you with the current shape your body is in?
- When was the last time you had a regular workout activity that you enjoyed?
- What could you do to be more active today that would not take much time?
- Can you do this alone, or would you prefer to exercise with someone else?
- How can you motivate yourself to stick with it . . . this time?

The Intellectual Slice

- What would a relaxing subject be today that would help you feel restful and at ease?
- Do you have a passion to learn or pursue such as reading, painting, photography, etc., that would get you excited?
- What is it you want to get out of this area of your life?
- Is there a subject in this area of your life that would benefit another part of your life?
- Is this something you would prefer to do by yourself, or would you prefer to participate in a group?

The Emotional Slice

- Do you think your emotions are under your control these days?
- Have your emotions helped you recently in the other areas of your life or not?
- What have you done, if anything, historically to manage and process your emotions in the other areas of your life?
- Would you be drawn to reading articles and books to spend some amount of time in this area and perhaps combining this with your Intellectual Slice?
- For you, would talking with someone skilled in this area be a better alternative?

The Spiritual Slice

- What has been your experience in this spiritual part of your life?
- How often have you practiced gratitude and slowed down to really breathe and rest?
- In your own life, do you feel that there is something much bigger in the world you need to connect with?
- What do you have faith in?
- Do you pray, meditate, connect with nature, etc., on a regular basis?

Once a highly active skier and tennis player, Gwen had forgotten why she no longer did any activities in her Physical Slice. She shook her head, smiled, and wondered, "When did that happen?"

Gwen had been a voracious reader of novels and nonfiction years ago but realized she had not read a book in over eight years, which she found disappointing. Now she read to keep up-to-date on her business sector. She said she was consistent about it, but also acknowledged that there were weeks when she read only when on an airplane.

Her Emotional and Spiritual Slices were all but vacant. The reason she gave herself 1 percent in each was because a few times a year she would attend holiday church services with her daughter and sometimes, but not often, would talk with a friend about her feelings about being a part-time mom while managing a demanding work and travel schedule.

The Seven-Slice exercise gave her pause. For the first time in a long while, she felt that she was taking stock of her life. She regretted that she had pretty much abandoned several of the Slices in her life, but at the same time, she appreciated the different perspectives gained through the exercise.

The first perspective was that she had been living her whole life as though it only consisted of her Family and Professional Slices. It was reassuring to her to think about taking some time, any time, to live in the other areas of her life to develop a better connection with herself. She realized that she didn't recognize or like her recent behavior, particularly around her family members. So we set a plan in place where she would use her strong organizing abilities to spend more time and energy in her underserved Slices. Here was Gwen's approach:

With time being precious, she sought ways to combine two or more Slices into one activity. She combined her Personal and Physical Slices by beginning to play tennis every Saturday. First, she played with a friend outside of work. After getting into better physical shape and rediscovering her tennis skills, she joined a local tennis club and contacted two old friends and one of her neighbors who also used to play. Interestingly, just the process of planning this new activity changed her energy level right away and boosted her attitude. She began to smile a bit more often.

Once she got into the rhythm of playing every weekend, she began to look forward to it, which was in marked contrast to how deflated she used to feel at the thought of spending her entire weekend just dealing with the problems in her Family Slice.

She did not see a reasonable way that she could increase her Emotional and Spiritual time commitment given the pressures she was under. So she decided that one thing she could do was to try to combine her Intellectual Slice with the Emotional and Spiritual Slices by reading for a few minutes a week at home.

It's key to have a realistic appreciation for what you know you won't or can't do when making a commitment in the individual Slices of your life. The goal is to start investing some time in nondominating Slices, but just as importantly, you want to keep those commitments. Though it does help in the short term to invest in each Slice, it is disappointing later when you abandon a commitment that benefited you because of time constraints or stress levels.

After Gwen had gotten back into tennis to address her Personal and Physical Slices, we decided she should look at the source of the stress in the Family Slice. The four major relationships that made up her Family Slice were all in disarray in one form or another. To find the solution with these relationships, she needed to understand how they became a problem in the first place to see if there was a pattern of behavior that could be identified and then addressed.

Gwen had come to understand that her bullying behavior in the office was a result of her inability to manage her Family Slice stress levels. So what to do about that? While no two people or situations are alike, you may recognize yourself or others in Gwen's family issues and how she managed her stress around them.

When I asked why these relationships had all deteriorated at the same time, she listed the issues. Gwen's mother constantly pressured Gwen to visit her in Germany more often. Gwen explained that her mother had never gotten over the fact that Gwen moved to the United States and didn't visit more than a couple of times a year. Since her mother was aging and in poor health, the pressure and the guilt hit all-time-high levels. It crushed Gwen more than she would let anyone know.

The relationship Gwen had with her daughter, Eva, was a combination of everything good and everything not so good in a mother-daughter relationship. Eva was a well-adjusted senior in high school with a stellar academic record. Like Gwen, she was very driven. According to Gwen, they had similar personalities. Most of the time, they got along extremely well. Periodically, they had titanic clashes that left both not speaking to each other for a day or two. This pattern had gone on for several years.

Eva decided that her college career would be in fashion. She found a school in Manhattan that she thought would give the best chance of breaking into that competitive industry.

During a stressless period, Gwen said she probably would have handled the college application conversations with a more measured approach, but instead, their dinner conversations now routinely erupted in tears, door slamming, and silence, with Eva's accusation of "You don't believe in me!" ringing in the kitchen. Mind you, Eva hadn't been accepted to fashion school—but the very discussion of her even applying sent Gwen into a fury.

Gwen's relationship with her ex-husband had never been great, but during this period, he was becoming increasingly difficult and making more demands regarding his time with Eva. He was also lobbying to reduce his alimony payments. Gwen had no interest in meeting his demands, which added another log to the fire. Her ex filed a legal complaint, and they were now back in court dealing with the financial aspect of the divorce. This was clearly creating tremendous fatigue and disappointment for Gwen during this already challenging time.

She had been in a relationship with her boyfriend, Damon, for about two years. It was a pleasant, caring relationship that had given Gwen the companionship and love that she was looking for during this time.

However, Damon had started putting pressure on Gwen to take the relationship to the next level. Their conversations around this subject were not going well. Both were frustrated with each other, and of course for Gwen, the timing was terrible. She could not understand why Damon, knowing the amount of stress she was under, was pressing her for a decision now.

She admitted she was behaving poorly. She was guilty of everything from erupting into angry outbursts to deliberately ignoring his texts and calls. She knew that these behaviors aggravated Damon. Afterward, she apologized out of guilt, but she repeated the behaviors the next time they clashed.

Her brother, George, was next on the family hit parade. George lived in Washington, DC, was married with two children, and had a very strained relationship with their mother in Germany. He visited her once every few years but refused to support their mother financially. Though Gwen tried to maintain a friendly relationship with her brother, his refusal to pitch in colored it all the same. When I asked her how much it bothered her, she indicated that it was not a subject she wanted to discuss. So I assumed it bothered her a great deal.

After several months, Gwen's office behavior had improved, and she was feeling a bit more at ease. I offered a suggestion to her. With her Family Slice still filled with stressful relationships, I asked her to consider the two Slices of her life that she had decided to put on hold due to the lack of time in her schedule.

We reviewed her answers to the Emotional and Spiritual Slice questions again. It was clear that if she were invested in those two Slices, she would be able to make decisions in other areas with much less angst and worry. Gwen was trying to deal with her upset emotions through activities that gave her a temporary respite and a better sense of harmony—however, the activities were not resolving the underlying issues. In each of her relationships in her Family Slice, we agreed that Gwen and everyone else involved would be much better off if she made firm decisions so everyone could move on with some level of acceptance. But while she agreed, she also asked how on earth that could happen in the middle of all this chaos.

So over the course of the next week, we explored the possibility of finding a good therapist who could walk her through the process of understanding how to think about her emotional life during this challenging period. What about the time factor? she asked. Surely, she didn't have time to add one more thing.

At this point, my response was simple and based completely in her reality. I asked, "What about the pain level?" She could not duck that one. Her emotional pain was severe, and she desperately wanted some relief.

In our previous sessions, Gwen mentioned that she was raised in a religious household and that she had faith in a spiritual power greater than the world. I asked, when was the last time she just sat and prayed or meditated with this greater power? It had been years, of course. In the spirit of full disclosure, I told her that my Spiritual Slice was an anchor for me and I believed in the power of prayer in my daily life. I explained that this Slice can take a lot of time or very little, but the benefits were almost always felt right away. She said she would think about it.

Within several weeks, Gwen fully accepted that she needed help, and she realized the help was all around her. She found a therapist that came highly recommended by her personal physician. They had met twice, and Gwen felt the sessions might help her. She was new to therapy, so did not quite get the process—but was pleased that she no longer felt as alone as she navigated through her challenges. Sitting and talking with someone, she reported, made her feel better in general.

She also started praying again. During her 40-minute commute, she turned off the car radio; and while she battled with distracting thoughts at first as she attempted to pray, after a week or so, she found her focus. She discovered that she was talking and asking for help and guidance more than praying, but like her therapy session, it helped her feel a sense of comfort in her mind and heart.

Now that Gwen was able to reach a more relaxed mindset, she began to tackle her family issues. Given her health situation, Gwen's mother agreed to live with Gwen and Eva for four months, an arrangement that not only brought the family together, but also gave her mother the opportunity to access the best medical advice in the United States. Eva and Gwen compromised over the choice of colleges by resolving that Eva would apply to both fashion and liberal arts schools and choose which school to attend after the acceptances were confirmed the next year. This was accomplished without the classic yell, scream, slam-door, and stop-speaking-for-two-days process that marked so much of their previous communication.

Gwen resigned herself to accept that the legal battle with her ex-husband simply had to run its course, and there was no point being angry and worrying about something she now had no control over.

I pointed out to Gwen that her shift in attitude came from somewhere—did she know where? She said that because she surrendered to the fact that she needed help, she felt like the pressure to be perfect just sort of fell away. The work with her therapist in the Emotional Slice, though going slowly, was beneficial because Gwen did not feel the need to "perform" in front of this person. It was a breath of fresh air for her to have someone in her life who was just there to help her.

Their work together was focusing on "ownership." They set up a system where Gwen could "measure," by using a specific set of criteria, the problems she "owned," the problems that she didn't own, and available solutions. This proved to be a moment of awakening, and it lessened the pressure she felt to perform every day in her Family and Professional Slices. She claimed this one step enabled her to look at life calmly, rather than feeling like life was always pursuing and pressuring her to do more and be better. She now felt she had the luxury to not worry about the legal battle and any possible negative outcomes it might bring.

Gwen's relationship with Damon took an interesting turn during this period. Though they were both divorced, had good careers, and should have felt "equal" in their relationship, Gwen always felt like she had to be in control. Damon had a habit of deferring to her in most decisions. While Gwen took advantage of that previously, she now decided that she wanted to change that power dynamic. So she tried to be as open as she could be with Damon.

Gwen asked Damon what he really wanted from her in this relationship. This pulled him up short, she said, and he tried to defer to her by saying, "Well, I want what you want." As you recall earlier, Gwen had said she preferred to be right versus happy—and ordinarily, she would have stepped in and given Damon the answer that would have benefited her. He would have shrugged and resentfully agreed. This time, she offered the floor to Damon by asking him again, what did he really want from her? Apparently, Damon was both surprised and flustered at this sudden change in the relationship dynamic. With some meandering, he was able to say he wanted to take the relationship to the next level, which included moving in together, sharing finances, and making a longer-term commitment.

To amplify how Gwen's attitude had adjusted, instead of simply providing an answer that she knew would disappoint Damon, she stated first that she totally understood and that it made perfect sense to her that he felt that way. She suggested that he deserved that kind of commitment, but she would not be able to go to the next level with him at this time because of the issues in her Family and Professional Slices of her life.

So Gwen offered Damon a solution. She stated that she could maintain the relationship at its current level for at least the rest of the year, and after that time, they could reevaluate where they both wanted to go. Or Damon could decide something different—it would be entirely up to him.

Gwen was identifying what her role was in this challenging moment. She realized that she did not have a problem with the relationship; Damon did. So rather than try to "fix it" for Damon, she determined that she could not provide a solution, and it was up to him to decide.

It was a difficult decision, certainly, but one that took a potentially highly emotional moment; and by choosing to not own it, Gwen was able to hand the problem back to the rightful owner. She had achieved her goal in the relationship. If they could be together without frustrating one another, then she would be happy to continue. But if the relationship was going to be fraught with continuous discord, then she would accept that and move on. Her peace of mind was worth it, she decided.

Ultimately, they both moved on, but amicably and with a level of emotional maturity that both appreciated. A true growth moment that was achieved without fear and undue stress. Gwen felt sad, but she knew in her heart that it was the best decision.

As far as her brother, George, was concerned, life was fine with him as long as Gwen was hosting their mother and he could minimize his involvement. A year prior, Gwen would have sought a solution to this by engaging George in a series of tense conversations to pressure him into living up to what she perceived as his family obligation to help support their mother.

Instead, with her newfound sense of what she could control and what she could not, Gwen decided that the relationship George had with their mother was his problem, not Gwen's. Further, she was able, over time, to accept that though she loved her brother, she could not really respect him. That enabled her to put the relationship in a new context that helped her not worry or think negatively about it any longer.

As Gwen moved forward in addressing these issues, which took over a year and a half, her work performance subtly improved. There were no significant moments or breakthrough meetings that turned the tide in her favor. She simply was able to slowly integrate herself and gain a new level of connection with herself.

Many years later, Gwen told me that she had learned it was important to achieve a perspective on a difficult issue, situation, or person first—rather than becoming stressed and upset. Today, she spends time in most of her Slices but does not really think about it because most of them are part of her lifestyle. She is grateful that she learned that there is a way to get through challenges without the anger, resentment, and frustration that had been a part of her prior life.

The Seven-Slice Method helped Gwen so much that she formed a women's business group where she introduced her own version of the method. Gwen said it was rewarding to see other people learn how to adapt to a method and discover a way to reduce their stress and handle the challenges of their lives with better, deeper understanding and more comfort.

CHAPTER SUMMARY

As we said at the outset of this chapter, your Family Slice is huge, and the amount of work you could do in this Slice to better manage your stress can seem overwhelming. Take heart from Gwen's story: engaging with all Seven Slices of your life will help you disperse and manage whatever stressors are at work in your Family Slice. Moreover, each problem has a beginning, middle, and end.

Not sure where to start? Ask yourself, "How present am I with the people in my life right now?" Are you able to give others your full attention, or are you unable to "turn off" your other thoughts? Why or why not?

People interact with their family differently. What things do you do well? What things are easy for you to do in the Family Slice of your life? What do you struggle with? We're not all good at the same things in our families. One sibling is often the nurturer, the next sibling is all about control, and the next is the comedian. Each of us seems to play a role, but it's very important to know when there are stress points, where they are coming from and why, and how you can play your role to maximize your chances of a reasonable outcome in any situation without being disruptive.

One thing to always remember is that the Family Slice is where we learn to be supportive—or not—to other people throughout our lives. One of the most important questions we can ask ourselves every day is, "Am I being as supportive to my family as I could be?" It seems a universal wish of every spouse is, "I wish my spouse would be more supportive." Asking yourself how supportive you are to family members once a day will almost certainly lead to a happier spouse and happier family life.

THE PROFESSIONAL SLICE

" **W**hat do you want to be when you grow up?"
We all remember being asked that question when we were young. From an early age, we're conditioned to see our career as a key part of our identity.

The Professional Slice is where you work and make your living or fulfill your responsibilities. It's where you build your professional career, business, or job. It starts with elementary, middle, and high school and then, for many, college and graduate school. Some go the vocational school route, while others learn through on-the-job experience. In any case, it's likely one of the Slices that claims the highest percentage of time in your life.

In this Slice, we must determine what we will do and how we will do it. Again, by need and design, we spend a lot of time at work. Many of us also spend a lot of time outside of work doing work-related activities so that we can accomplish our tasks, projects, and goals successfully.

Since the beginning of human history, people have had to provide for their families and themselves. Money is what keeps a roof over your head and food on the table. By design, professionals who command high salaries, senior titles, and career prestige must invest more time and energy in developing skills and keeping those skills up-to-date than people in other fields. But even if you're not after the corner office, performing skilled work and earning money is the means by which people provide security for themselves and their families. That makes the stakes pretty high. It's no wonder that this Slice can so easily dominate people's lives.

WORK AND PURPOSE

But our professional lives aren't just about survival and security. A wonderful book called *Working: People Talk About What They Do All Day and How They Feel About What They Do* by Studs Terkel was very popular in the 1970s. It is a collection of interviews about people, their jobs, and how they feel about working at those jobs.

Two interesting conclusions came out of those interviews. One was that people who found satisfaction in their work were generally much more productive than those who did not. The second was, for many people, work was more than a way to earn their daily bread—it provided meaning in their lives.

Simple but profound, Terkel's conclusions fundamentally answer the question, "Why do we go to work?" So this Slice is powerful on many levels. Not surprisingly then, the stress produced here has a powerful impact on our whole lives.

In addition to generating the money we need, work contributes a great deal to our personal development, if we let it. In our profession or job, we are all free to decide what makes us satisfied and what does not. As I have explained many times to clients, you control your own decision-making. For some people, work is a means to an end. Their paycheck enables them to do what they really want to do with their life. If you identify with this stance, you're less likely to be dissatisfied if your Professional Slice doesn't speak to your life's purpose. You've got other things going on. For others, however, their job is connected to something they love, something that drives them. These people are more likely to have overlap (or perceived overlap) between their Professional Slice and their Intellectual Slice, their Personal Slice, or other Slices.

My observation: most people over the age of 42 who "plateau" in their careers do so because they've met their own expectations. They say to themselves: "I have a well-paying job, I have the family I want, the vacation time I want, and a 401(k)." They've achieved their goals. In contrast, people who keep building their careers past that age haven't met their own expectations; they have more goals to achieve. What about you? Do you see your work as a means to an end or as part of your life's purpose? Identifying which stance you fall into is important, because that can help guide how you attend the Seven Slices of your life and how you can find satisfaction on your terms.

Something that I hear a great deal in my work is that people want their work to have a purpose and make a difference in the world. While people said similar things years ago, it tended to be more of a hope than a need. Today, it seems to be a prerequisite.

For many of us, the Professional Slice marks the first time that our career success and wealth get measured together. As our work performance increases and we contribute more to our organization, we usually make more money. Therefore, our motivations become quite clear. And we learn our employer's motivations, as well. For instance, your employer might really expect you to step up (which may be welcomed by you or not). When the motivations of you and your employer map closely to each other, you have a good match. When the motivations are in conflict, then we experience discord on both sides of the relationship.

DO YOU HAVE A HEALTHY RELATIONSHIP WITH YOUR WORK?

Sometimes I'll ask my clients, "How would you describe your relationship with your work?" The answers range across the board.

All of us have a relationship with our work. It is just like any other relationship in our lives. Some say their relationship is "just OK." Some love the relationship. Some see it as a means to an end. Some are unhappy and frustrated. Some have found the passionate relationship they always wanted. Some seek a more purposeful work relationship but haven't found it yet.

The point is, your work relationship is like any other; it needs to be nurtured. So how we think about our work matters because we spend so much time in it over our lifetime.

THE PROFESSIONAL'S DILEMMA

Several clients over the years have discussed the professional's dilemma openly. If you don't struggle and compete in business, the people in your family may not have the things that money can buy and that you feel they deserve. If you want your family to live in a fine home in a good neighborhood with great schools and have a good social life, you need to generate a sizable income. Yet if you overinvest in your career, there are often unintended consequences, such as becoming disconnected from yourself, your family, your friends, and your soul.

On the other hand, investing less of yourself in your career can leave unfulfilled potential and achievement. Further, society tends to assign our stature based on the progress we make in our Professional Slice. Hence, the pressure and stress many feel to keep up with the expectations we set for ourselves are often based on what we think will impress others.

All of this results in what I like to call a "natural tension," in that both sides have value; you need to manage them effectively to achieve your goals. For example, if your expectations and your employer's expectations are in conflict, something must give. I once worked with a client whose employer was not meeting her expectations. Her company wanted her to "stay in her lane." My client, however, wanted to achieve more and rise to a higher level. Ultimately, she quit and moved to a company that had higher expectations for her.

Through trial and error, I have found that the process that seems to be the most efficient and least harmful to address the professional's dilemma is making sure the person lives in all Seven Slices of his or her life.

THE SPECIAL CHALLENGE OF THE PROFESSIONAL SLICE

At work, there are always eyes on you. It's a true performance Slice, and if you do well, you receive financial rewards. If you fall short, then your pay could very well go down, or you could even lose your job.

Everyone must work with other people. If you're normally a pleasant person and suddenly you become moody, rude, detached, dismissive, or just not present, others will notice. And if your superiors notice, then the conversation behind your back could easily shift to, "I thought so-and-so was a fit here, but maybe not."

Given all the busyness and pressure that's become intrinsic to so many workplaces, it's easy for the Professional Slice to dominate your life. However, if you catch yourself thinking, "No, no, my job is everything"—or acting as though it is—that's a problem that can often reflect that you're not managing your job stress effectively.

CHECKING IN WITH YOUR PROFESSIONAL SLICE

Since work is where many of us spend the largest percentage of our time, it can be tough to know when you've got a healthy relationship with your Professional Slice (especially since it seems like being stressed and busy is "normal").

Here are some signs you have a healthy Professional Slice:

- Even during the most stressful and worst times at work, you leave work (and the stress that comes with it) at work.
- Your temperament is consistent, even during periods of acute stress and pressure.
- You feel as though you have a good mix of success and challenges that reward and motivate you every day.
- Your coworkers report that your temperament is steady and you're easy to work with.

Of course, no one's Professional Slice is perfect. It's normal to find many things in your professional life that are going well and many things that need work. But when both motivate you, that's when you know your Professional Slice is in good shape. It's usually obvious when your Professional Slice isn't going well—again, you've got eyes on you regularly rating and evaluating your performance. Here are some common signs indicating you need to work on how you manage your stress:

- You feel physically and/or mentally fatigued.
- You're unable to concentrate.
- You're unable to truly pay attention to those around you.
- You're unable to disengage from work, even when you're around your loved ones.
- You find yourself swinging high or low easily—a good performance review makes you feel like you're on top of the world; a missed deadline feels like the entire world is crashing down.
- Your worry and anxiety about business issues steal time away from your loved ones.
- Your loved ones tell you that you're being short, rude, or just not present with them.
- Your coworkers have started to ask questions such as "Is everything OK?" or making observations such as "You look exhausted."

While everyone might have an off day here and there, if you consistently experience any of the above, the Seven-Slice Method can be an effective intervention.

THE STRESS CYCLE

So many people just grit their teeth and plow forward during periods of acute stress and end up suffering long term as a result.

Again, a few of the symptoms that let you know stress is having an effect on you include physical or mental fatigue, the inability to concentrate, and complaints from your loved ones about the length or quality of time that you spend with them. These three are the most prevalent that I have witnessed in my work with business executives at every organizational level.

It's easy to fall into a cycle of highs and lows in the Professional Slice where the negative symptoms show up during the highly stressful period. Then the circumstance passes, life goes back to normal, and the symptoms disappear—for a while. You're relaxed, and everyone likes being around you again.

But then a different stressful circumstance enters the picture and the same acute stress symptoms make a return visit—and often introduce a new symptom, such as shoulder pain—and we rinse and repeat. The physical and emotional impact of this high-and-low cycle can make you feel as though you're constantly in catch-up mode and never ahead of the game. The Seven-Slice Method can help you break that destructive pattern of highs and lows.

LEVERAGE THE SKILLS YOU ALREADY HAVE TO WORK TOWARD HARMONY

For you professionals struggling with this Slice, there are two skills that can make a huge difference while executing the Seven-Slice Method. The good news is, you're likely already using those skills every day. And even if you struggle with them, the Seven-Slice Method is a great practice arena to build them up.

The first is prioritization. Prioritizing effectively allows you to understand the difference between being busy and being productive. We all have 50 things that need to be done today, but how many of us know the top 5 things that must be done? And how many can pick the correct 5 that will impact the other 45 in small or large ways?

Prioritizing is one of the secrets to success in any business, job, or profession. It answers the question, "What are the five most important tasks that need to be done that will impact the people, the process, or the execution?" When you get the right answer, you cannot fail. Using the skill of prioritizing in determining how to live in all Seven Slices is critical to ensure harmony in your life.

The second skill is time management. If anything contributes to the feeling of being stressed, it is time. Learning how to get things done with the amount of time you have is the heartbeat of time management.

One thing I have always noted about successful people: they have no more time than the rest of us, and yet they get more done and take on more responsibility. How is that possible? Typically, they identify what needs to be done first, second, and third. In addition, they understand they don't have to do the whole thing themselves. They can delegate parts or ask for help, a practice that then allows them to take on more responsibility because they are not doing 100 percent of anything. At the same time, they know they own the result, so they monitor progress and deliver on time.

SLICE CASE STUDY: JANE

Jane was an ambitious woman in her forties living in Manhattan and in a serious relationship with a successful attorney in the city. She had recently made partner at a small investment bank and loved her work. The managing partner there was also Jane's mentor, and Jane strived to follow in her footsteps. She was very analytical, focused on creating value in the firm's portfolio companies, and dedicated to the firm's investors. She also had top-notch people skills.

While everything was going well in her Professional Slice, Jane's Family Slice hit a crossroad, and she had to make some decisions. Jane and her partner had been together for two years and now lived together. Jane knew what she wanted: a committed relationship and marriage. She also wanted to have a child.

John, her partner, however, was older than Jane and considered their current situation ideal for him. Further, he was under a great deal of pressure at his law firm and kept putting off any big decisions concerning his relationship with Jane. As far as having children, he was ambivalent about the whole idea and hadn't thought it through completely. As he was fond of saying, "Children are forever."

Jane realized this was a deal breaker. She and John wanted different things out of life. Given that fact, and that the big life-changing things that she desired were time-sensitive, she ended the relationship.

While this was the right decision, the experience of breaking up and moving out was a bitter and extremely stressful experience for them both. Less than four months later, Jane decided that she would have a child on her own and began the exhaustive process of adopting a baby.

As someone who was accustomed to taking on difficult challenges and succeeding, it seemed perfectly logical to Jane that an adoption could be achieved within a year. She looked forward to the upcoming changes in her life. She was a classic process thinker, and she hadn't given much thought to the emotional toll her decisions might have on her.

Soon after, her coworkers noticed a marked change in Jane's behavior. Her overall attitude became abrupt and tense. For instance, during a company management meeting, she repeatedly interrupted the CFO to ask uncomfortable direct questions about the numbers. It was clear too that the questions should have been handled in private. In the past, Jane had been particularly good at reading the room—now, however, she plowed forward even when people were shifting uncomfortably in their chairs and exchanging shocked glances.

This was a huge problem. In the investment banking business, you're asking people to entrust their business to you so you can help them raise money or help them sell their company. Jane's people skills were essential to her success—and people noticed when her performance fell short.

Jane's behavior prompted the managing partner to call her in for a discussion. Jane sat and listened but was rather cavalier about the situation. She was just going through a "few things at home," she assured the managing partner. After a pause, Jane outlined the issues she was facing in her personal life. However, she said she would be back on the beam immediately.

The managing partner pointed out that Jane's challenges outside of work would be a lot for anyone to navigate. She suggested that Jane get some help to manage everything going on.

Jane politely said no, that wasn't necessary and that she would handle the situation on her own. The meeting ended on her assurance that all would be well.

It has been my experience that when we decide to deflect or deny the reality others point out to us, it never ends particularly well.

Sure enough, in the weeks after this discussion took place, Jane's behavior at the office did not improve, and her job performance started to suffer. Her disappointment and frustration in herself compounded her stress.

In addition, the adoption process was more challenging than she had anticipated due to the fact she was a single parent competing against married couples. The "competition" aspect (in which she was at a perceived disadvantage) intensified her emotions.

It was at this time that I was asked to get involved. I had been working with the other partners in the firm on their company portfolio personnel issues and was familiar with the firm and its culture.

Over the next several months, Jane and I talked about the challenges and problems she was dealing with. My role was to see if we could find some sort of balance so Jane could be more comfortable and get some relief from the stressful situation she was dealing with every day. As she shared what was going on, it became clear that Jane was getting hit from both sides of her life: the external circumstances were causing stress, and at the same time, she was beating herself up about how she was reacting to those circumstances.

It was clear Jane was living almost exclusively in the two primary Slices of her life—Professional and Family. Not only that, but those two Slices were now in competition with each other. Without some adjustment soon, a positive outcome appeared doubtful.

After we spent some time walking through the Seven-Slice Method and the impact it might have on her current situation, Jane wanted to give it a shot.

Since we all learn differently, Jane thought it would be best for her to evaluate her five dormant Slices first: her Physical, Personal, Intellectual, Emotional, and Spiritual Slices.

- **Physical Slice.** Due to her busy and stressful schedule, Jane had not worked out or exercised in about a year. She felt lethargic and tired most days.
- **Personal Slice.** Jane did not have a particularly large number of social contacts, and she had all but ignored her small circle of friends over the

past year or so. Although she was not an extrovert, she missed socializing, particularly lately.

- **Intellectual Slice.** Her curiosity levels were entirely focused on her work and family situation, which left no time for other intellectual pursuits. Further, intellectual matters had all but drifted away from her conscious thoughts, which she found both surprising and disappointing.

- **Emotional Slice.** As far as her emotions were concerned, she was too stressed and consumed with her daily tasks to pay much attention to this part of her life.

- **Spiritual Slice.** And finally, having been raised in a Protestant faith, she had slowly drifted away from attending church years ago and had not pursued this part of her life in a decade.

It was eye-opening for Jane to acknowledge these dormancies in her life, and to see the extent to which her Family and Professional Slices had crowded everything else out.

Next, we did a deeper dive into her dominant Slices. Since so many people struggle with these dominant Slices, there are specific questions I ask to help get to the bottom of why they react to certain situations the way they do:

The Family Slice

1. In your family, are love, appreciation, and affection easily expressed?
2. Is the time you spend in this part of your life enjoyable for you?
3. Did you learn from your family how to handle stress and crisis well?
4. Did you learn boundaries in your family, and do you set them in your own family today?
5. In your family, is conflict and learning from it a priority?

The Professional Slice

1. Is your professional occupation providing you the challenges you are looking for in your career growth?
2. Do you think your professional life is helping you fulfill your purpose, or is it a means to an end?
3. Are you your authentic self in this area of your life or not?
4. Is integrity and honesty a part of your life in this area of your life?

5. Does your professional life build patience or impatience for you in the rest of your life?

Obviously, these questions are not meant to be answered in one sitting. What Jane and others have found is that the answers start to come in a general form initially, but then begin to take real shape as they think about them more deeply in the context of their entire life.

After analyzing her Seven Slices, Jane thought she found an insight that eventually helped her find the key to reducing her stress level and improving her daily attitude.

Jane realized that her Professional Slice was the dominant force in her time and life—to the point where it was driving almost all her behaviors in every other part of her life. She realized after reviewing each Slice that she was taking the focus and skills that made her successful in her Professional Slice and force-applying them to her Family Slice.

As she reviewed the questions in the Family Slice, a couple of things hit home. The first thing she noted was that while the damage was done already at home, she could learn from the past to ensure the future might be less riddled with stress and acrimony. Second, like most people, she knew her work-life balance was not good, but she did not realize that she was spending so little time in the other five Slices of her life.

Another question I like to ask (not only others but myself as well) is, "Why do you think that you ignore an area of your life and not notice it until a Method like this comes along that gets you to examine your life?"

Jane's response was quick and accurate. She said the sheer busyness of her life coupled with the financial rewards coming out of her Professional Slice allowed her to easily ignore the rest of her life.

I think this is an important question for every professionally successful person to consider. So many times, we put pressure on ourselves to measure up to a series of extremely high standards that are either set by others or set by us. And measuring up to those standards becomes an all-consuming passion that often extinguishes other elements of our lives.

Interestingly, Jane's answers to the Family Slice questions revealed a lot about how she managed her Professional Slice. Take a look at her answers:

1. *In your family, are love, appreciation, and affection easily expressed?*
   Jane was an only child, and her parents divorced when she was 10 years old. She lived with her mother but remained close to her father.

Her parents were successful professionals and expected Jane to excel and be the best she could be. However, according to Jane, her mother and father were quite different from each other. Her father was a lawyer who was gregarious and charming. He never pushed Jane, although he expected her to achieve due to her natural talents and abilities. His philosophy was, *For those much has been given, much is expected.* Her mother, a college professor of English, was introverted, quiet, and a bit of a taskmaster. Jane was a bright student and a good athlete, so her mother instilled in Jane the need to excel at both.

Though Jane knew her mother loved her, her mother was a bit detached, and affection came in the form of praise for a job well done versus a spontaneous hug or warm words. Jane shrugged when she explained that, as if to say, "Oh well..."

2. *Is the time you spend in this part of your life enjoyable for you?*
Jane's answer here was conditional, meaning it depended on what was going on and the circumstance at the time. After she became an adult, her interactions with her parents diminished; she saw them mainly during holidays or family events. She enjoyed seeing them and catching up, but they never did much together outside of the immediate function.

3. *Did you learn from your family how to handle stress and crisis well?*
Her comments here were clear. She learned precisely how to handle stress and crisis: *make a plan; work through it; don't complain because others have it a lot worse than you!* Once again, Jane laughed as she reviewed this with me, "Well, I guess I learned that pretty well!" I pointed out that this activity-based approach to managing stress and pressure is quite common. She understood but remembered she would have liked to have had a bit more emotional support as she handled the challenges of school and college. I pointed out that sometimes stress and pressure cannot be resolved with an activity plan and a "head's-down" approach. Jane simply smiled and shook her head.

4. *Did you learn boundaries in your family, and do you set them in your own family today?*
On this question, Jane could not have been more clear. She grew up successfully, with boundaries set at every point in her life, or so it seemed. She agreed that she became an obedient child as a result, and as an adult, she claimed to impose very defined boundaries. She

felt that rules and boundaries actually created a sense of freedom and time management.

In her family, conflict was avoided. When conflict did surface, it was handled with facts and decisions and little or no negotiation or discussion. Again, for Jane, these were the expectations, and an alternative method was never discussed, even to this day.

After discussing her answers, we looked at the other Slices of her life for the purpose of measuring how much time she was spending in them. Through the Seven-Slice Pie (shown in Chapter 10), we tried to attach the percentages of time she spent in each of the Seven Slices. Here were her results after several attempts to get it as accurate as possible:

- Family Slice: 10 percent
- Professional Slice: 80 percent
- Personal Slice: 2 percent
- Physical Slice: 2 percent
- Intellectual Slice: 2 percent
- Emotional Slice: 2 percent
- Spiritual Slice: 2 percent

After understanding how she spent her time, "I suggested that even though the source of her stress was the Family Slice, she spent the bulk of her time each day in the Professional Slice, and so wouldn't it make sense that she tried to work the stress out in that Slice first?"

It was clear that the other Slices were not available to help filter that stress and provide a level of perspective for her life in the Professional Slice to remain positive and productive. It seemed simple to Jane. She wondered, when did this all happen to her?

Again, I reminded her that she was not alone. Many successful people have profile percentages like hers. The key was not to judge herself but rather to make a decision about how to activate the other Slices of her life to help her deal with the stress in her life—now, and going forward, since stress will always be part of her life. Jane was open to developing a plan to use the other areas of her life to help with her stress, as long as it didn't impinge on her Professional and Family Slices. It took some time, but we were able to put a plan together that started slowly but ultimately worked for Jane. With the lack of time being a big challenge, we settled on an approach that combined two Slices into one activity. She combined her Physical and Personal Slices by deciding to walk home from her office in the city instead of using the Metro. It was a 30-to-40-minute walk in decent weather, and she committed (after a suggestion) to not take any calls for business while she walked. She would only speak with a friend while on the walk or just think and tune out the day's pressures.

As a fact-based thinker, Jane imposed a four-week deadline to determine if this approach would yield positive results. If combining these two Slices produced some improvement in her reducing the stress level and her work performance improved, then we would look at the other Slices.

After three weeks, we had our findings. By then it was spring in Manhattan. The weather had cooperated, and Jane, after a week or so, looked forward to her walks home. She found it gave her time to unplug and transition into the evening. She managed to schedule two calls a week with friends whom she had not seen in over a year. She indicated that she felt better, and she used the word "lighter." She also noted that her breathing was deeper and slower from the exercise of walking for that length of time without stopping, except at the traffic intersections.

I asked if her stress levels were lower since she started this routine in the two Slices of her life. She said, "Absolutely." I pointed out to her that there were no significant changes in her life circumstances, and in fact, the adoption process was getting more complicated. Further, the deal flow was increasing in her work, which meant that she was busier than usual. Despite all this, she said she felt better overall, and though she wouldn't call herself happy, she was not nearly as worried and stressed out.

I wondered how she was being perceived at the office now that we were several weeks into this new routine. She wasn't sure, but she thought things might be better in that everyone was acting as though things were back to "business as usual."

I checked with her coworkers on an informal basis, and they all said the same thing: Jane seemed a bit more relaxed and easier to deal with, even though the workload hadn't changed. She was still a bit detached but was an improved version of herself over the past month or so. When I shared that with her, she was genuinely pleased and said she wanted to think about the next steps in this Seven-Slice Method.

We tried to make a plan that would allow her to devote a sliver of time to her other three Slices given her busy schedule. Her three remaining Slices were Intellectual, Emotional, and Spiritual. How would she address these three areas of her life with no additional time available—or so it appeared?

Where there is a will, there is a way.

After several frustrating starts, Jane came up with a simple plan that, again, did not require a lot of time. Jane decided to invest 15 minutes every night before going to bed to read. Being a purpose-driven person, she would read with a purpose. She decided to focus on self-improvement books first. I gave her a list of authors that I thought Jane would be drawn to, and as luck would have it—she was! It took some time and a few fits and starts to make the 15-minute reading exercise part of her new routine. As we all have been told, it takes 21 days to form a habit,[1] and for Jane with her fits and starts, it took a few months to establish her new reading habit.

Fortunately, the first book she read grabbed her attention, and she saw many qualities and characteristics in herself as she read about what other people went through to find themselves and their way to personal growth. The book provided her with a new perspective almost right away. It is quite a moment when you sit by yourself and read about people who went through what you are going through right now and you realize, "I'm not alone."

Jane found this particularly welcoming and comforting. She had an insecurity streak going far back in her life and always wondered if there was something wrong with her or if other people were somehow better. That was the first learning she gained when she added 15 minutes of reading to the end of her day. Quite the return on her investment.

Over the next several months, Jane moved closer to adopting a child while she continued to perform at a high level in her job. Both issues dominated her waking moments, but she was able to process the intensity and stress that each produced, so she was calmer and more reflective than at any other time in her life. She still worried and was occasionally withdrawn in the office—particularly now that she was paying attention to other areas of her life—but she was still a valued member of the team. She received word that she was eligible to be a mother through adoption, and a year later she became the mother of a one-year-old child.

Shortly after the adoption went through, I saw Jane and inquired if she was still utilizing the Seven-Slice Method and if it still was having a positive impact on her life. She was happy to report that though her life was hectic and stressed, she did not feel that way herself. She had childcare assistance, and her mother was pitching in to help. Jane was genuinely excited about her child and the direction of her life.

Interestingly, when we first examined her Slices, Jane spent no time at all with her Spiritual Slice. She now informed me that she had begun attending a Protestant church that was right around the corner from her home in the city. She found the sermons to be thought provoking, and attending the Sunday morning services gave her time to just think and pray. Although the impact on her was slow in developing, she felt good that she was making an effort to raise her daughter in a religious faith.

Hearing this, I pointed out that Jane had been touching all Seven Slices of her life for a while now. I asked, what impact did she think it had on her life? She paused and explained that she could not believe how investing a little time in touching the Personal, Physical, Intellectual, Emotional, and Spiritual Slices had enriched her life. Her health, mental stamina, and personal well-being were better, and she was learning to look for happiness rather than waiting for it to show up.

My sense of Jane was that she found a rhythm for living her very hectic, competitive, and fulfilling life by not letting life run her, but rather the other way around. She wasn't trying to change her life; instead, she was trying to live in a way where she could find some ease rather than dis-ease with the circumstances and people she encountered. Her life was not perfect, but she felt better about it and was confident that as more problems were surely to come her way, she believed now that she could handle them without the fear of falling apart at the seams.

CHAPTER SUMMARY

Ultimately if you live long enough and retire or just stop working, you end up with Six Slices, not Seven. Your Professional Slice may demand a high percentage of your time now, but it will eventually retire or disappear one way or the other.

On the other hand, your Family Slice lasts your entire life. So many successful professionals tell themselves, "I'll get to spend more time with my family after I retire or slow down." But sometimes it's too late. They've missed too much.

Similarly, many people reach retirement and say, "Now what?" They hadn't kept up with their own interests along the way, and so when they exit the workforce, they feel lost.

If you allow your Professional Slice to dominate your life completely, there may be consequences down the road.

There is tremendous value in investing in all Seven of your Slices. By making sure that you touch your other Slices consistently, you're more likely to be present and available with your family—even when work is at its most hectic.

And furthermore, keeping up with your other Slices means that you're keeping up with other interests in your life. You won't retire and say, "Now what?" because you've been maintaining a life outside of work all along.

Many people tell me it feels "freeing" to know where the Professional Slice fits in their whole life rather than trying to look at it in isolation. Take your temperature from time to time and make sure that your Professional Slice isn't dominating most of your time. It's an easy check that will signal you to dial down your Professional Slice and dial up your interests and time in your other Six Slices.

THE PERSONAL SLICE

The Personal Slice, at first blush, can be challenging to define, understand, and implement in a way that allows you to harmonize it with your other six Slices.

This Slice is first and foremost all about you.

Your Personal Slice is filled with possibilities for you to explore. The possibilities only require your interest and energy. Where you put both is entirely up to you. It is a place of personal freedom. But proceed thoughtfully. How you invest in your Personal Slice is critical if you are going to find the harmony in the other areas or Slices of your life.

THE PERSONAL SLICE IS A PLACE
FOR PERSONAL FREEDOM

A lot of people who are under stress claim (or unconsciously believe) they don't have the freedom to control their own life: "I have a heavy-duty job with lots of responsibilities. I have children I must take care of, family and friends whom I need to support as they go through challenges—I just don't have the freedom to live my own life the way I want to. There's just no time for me."

Many people feel that way from time to time, but it's important that you don't completely surrender yourself to your responsibilities and obligations. You can think of the Personal Slice as your escape hatch. This is the one Slice per week that you and you alone control. That gives you freedom for that period of time to do something for your own benefit that does not have to involve anything or anyone else.

Some people react with surprise at this idea—as though they need someone's permission to spend time on themselves! Most of us tend to seek out routines in our lives that leave little room for personal interests, so it is easy to leave this Slice behind and only realize later that it is missing in action.

This is your chance to pursue your curiosity and interests that lie outside the Family and Professional Slices of your life. As the years go by, many people spend less and less time with just themselves. It's easy to become too busy working, providing, nurturing, and caring for others. But occasionally you need to hit the pause button for a bit and just pursue you.

Let's talk about how people use this Slice in a positive way that harmonizes with the rest of their lives. This Slice allows you to pursue what interests you. It might be physical activities such as running, working out, or training for a marathon. It can be calming and relaxing activities like gardening or a casual hobby. It can be as simple as reading the books that have been on your list for years. It can also be purposeful and deliberate, such as deciding to pursue volunteering for a nonprofit that has meaning to you.

You might decide to pursue a dedicated commitment like learning a new language or a musical instrument. Or you might like to get back into acting, which you enjoyed in high school or college. Towns and cities have local community theaters that are always looking for talented people to give their time for an artistic performance.

Perhaps something dramatic like climbing mountains captures your interest and curiosity. One of the most interesting pursuits I encountered was that of a client who always wondered if he would like ice climbing, a sport where you literally scale an ice wall while tied to a rope. One false move, and off you go. Yikes! He pursued it and loves it to this day.

For intense people, their Personal Slice might match their intensity, whereas someone who's more relaxed might want to pursue a more contemplative activity. Some people love hot-air ballooning, while others are afraid of heights. The key is to have something in this Slice that's yours.

Beyond these types of activities and hobbies, there are many other pursuits that can address what you need to receive from the time spent in the Personal Slice. Often, you can combine these pursuits with other Slices of your life, which makes the results even more interesting.

For example, take leisure activities. Research shows that leisure activities help our physical and mental well-being.[1] Leisure activities could mean doing absolutely nothing—for instance, lying in a hammock outside for a half an hour—or they may have a more physical component. Think about activities you would enjoy that you could also combine with your Physical Slice. For example, bicycling, bowling, horseback riding, golfing, walking, skating, and swimming are enjoyable to most people and provide physical exercise. However, it's fine to spend time in your Personal Slice on less physical activities, such as painting, drawing, reading, listening to music, or meditating.

People who have not spent much time in their Personal Slice can find activating this aspect of their life a bit challenging. The rewards are clear: the Personal Slice activities described here help to renew a person's spirit, improve a person's health, and provide perspectives. The consequences of not spending enough time here is that you spend even more time in the family and work area. That's obviously important—but so are you. The initiative that you take in the Personal Slice rewards you by improving how you feel about yourself, your world, and the other six Slices of your life.

Time, of course, is the enemy for all of us in finding space in our lives to spend on ourselves. For some, it almost feels "selfish" to spend time on ourselves when there is so much else that must be done. But spending time in the Personal Slice helps you to be more available to the people and circumstances that take up most of the rest of your time. When you are simply enjoying and relaxing, your mind and body are no longer in fight/protect mode—and that allows you to renew and recharge. The gift of rest and perspective delivers physical and emotional benefits for all of us.

Some describe the time spent in their Personal Slice as being peaceful—which is what allows them to distance themselves from their stress. What a quality to have at the ready when you need to just stop, relax, and take a break from your everyday stress.

Now, to reiterate an earlier comment, you can combine this Slice with several other Slices to be more efficient and address the time management issues we all struggle to harness.

For instance, many people enjoy building small projects at home in the garage or a separate workshop. Teaching your children the same hobby combines your Personal with your Family Slice in one activity. Other hobbies, such as knitting or crafting, can be done alone or with friends. The feeling of warmth and friendship as you relax together can contribute to both your Personal and your Emotional Slice. Some of the most popular personal activities concern connecting with nature. For instance, you might pick up photography, bird watching, or camping on your own or with members of your family and/or friends.

HOW MUCH TIME DO YOU NEED?

The question people often asked when they begin to think about their Personal Slice is, "How much time do I need there?" Meaning, "Is there a certain amount of time I must commit to get something out of it?" The answer depends on what you choose as your personal activity, to some degree. Picking up ice climbing, for instance, will require training, tools, and potential travel and ultimately may take up a great deal of time. But regardless of the activity, the interest and energy level you bring to it will largely dictate the amount of time you need to devote to the activity.

Let's take meditation as an example. This is a Personal Slice and/or an Emotional Slice activity based on what you want to get out of it. Meditation can be as simple as quieting yourself, slowing your breathing, and listening to your own breath. At that level, you and I could do that for five minutes a day, every day, and feel a brief but beneficial sense of calm from those few minutes.

Someone else with a different motive and intent could invest a great deal in meditating. As experts have noted, meditation can be a lifelong endeavor where there is almost no end to what you can discover and learn.[2] If one wanted to pursue that goal, then the amount of time would be fairly significant. I know people who spend an hour a day, every day, meditating. They could not live without it. I know others who meditate a few times a week for a few minutes and claim it calms and soothes them. Both receive the benefit from their own investment. The point is, any amount of time that you invest in your Personal Slice is fine if it coincides with your interest level and commitment and you receive a benefit.

MORE INSPIRATION FOR
YOUR PERSONAL SLICE

There's no right or wrong way to spend time in your Personal Slice. One person might think, "I would really love to go to a movie by myself." Why don't you go do that? Once a week, once a month, go to town. But that same activity might be a form of punishment for someone else.

Be aware that you might have to overcome some of your own excuses, as well. For instance, you might be interested in volunteering at a soup kitchen but feel that you just don't have time. Before writing the activity off, give the organization a call and ask how you can help and when does it need help. Many organizations that rely on volunteers will have ideas for how busy people can pitch in.

I had an older client tell me that she really loved babies, but she didn't have any grandchildren. When I discovered that she also attended church regularly, I pointed out that most churches have nurseries or need volunteers to hold crying babies during the service. Don't give up easily—there is likely a way to find an outlet for your interest.

Your calendar can be a helpful partner. For instance, one of my clients and her husband both worked from home. They noticed that their video-conference meetings were always scheduled back to back to back, and so they both felt exhausted by the end of the day. Their solution was to put a "meeting" on their calendar for an hour starting at 5:00 or 5:30 p.m. Then the two of them would use that time to go for a walk around the neighborhood together. That was their way of being in their Personal Slice, but it was also a little bit of Physical and Family. Moreover, it helped their relationship because they were both checking out and refreshing for an hour and not taking care of anyone else. They were just with each other for an hour.

WHAT ABOUT MOVIES, BINGE-WATCHING, AND SOCIAL MEDIA?

Many people in pursuit of an escape during the day turn to binge-watching television shows, watching movies, or spending time on social media. Could these activities count toward your Personal Slice?

The answer is that it depends. Check in with yourself after spending time online or watching one of your favorite shows. Do you feel refreshed? Recharged? If so, then yes, these activities are serving your Personal Slice.

If, however, you stop scrolling or click off the TV feeling the same or even more drained and worn out, then you may want to rethink the amount of time you spend there.

WHAT ABOUT CREATIVITY?

In the world of behavioral science, it is said every left-handed person has a creative skill.[3] Personally, I have found this to be true. When I meet with a left-handed person, I always ask about the person's creative ability: "So what do you do with it?" Most have an answer. Some sing, some paint, some create with ceramics, some build fantastic gardens, and on and on. Very few let their skill lie fallow. It's funny to me because the world is built for right-handed people. This is sort of like the lefty's revenge.

So in their Personal Slice, with this creative skill in them, there is no negotiating around, "Do I use it or not?" It is part of who they are as people. It would be like telling them not to eat breakfast again. It just makes total sense to them to create, because the intrinsic benefit they receive helps them to develop other areas of their lives. Many told me that exercising their creative skill provides them with the simple joy of doing something well and provides benefits to others who enjoy listening to their music, appreciating their art, or viewing their garden.

So that got me wondering one day. Could anyone be creative as long as the person gave it a try? Remember this definition of art? It is whatever you think it is. Remember when Andy Warhol painted the iconic Campbell Soup cans? I am not suggesting you and I can start producing iconic art any time soon, but I do believe most people can be creative in their Personal Slice. And as for you right-handed people, take heart—the world was designed for you. If a creative pursuit captures your interest, there's nothing stopping you.

POSSIBILITY THINKING

Creativity requires many things, but it seems to revolve around possibility thinking and personality. Thinking about possibilities is always a positive notion. It allows your mind to explore and think about what interests you. Sometimes creativity is born of necessity, as is seen all the time in emergency and crisis situations where people devise practical solutions to daunting problems. For example, during the Covid-19 crisis, food was sitting on farms with no means to transport it to market and get it to hungry people who had suddenly lost their jobs. One man devised a creative solution that entailed launching a small band of volunteers who utilized trucks to haul the food from the farms to the most heavy-hit cities in the United States.[4]

If you are curious by nature, then creative thinking will likely fit into your life fairly easily. Curious people tend to be comfortable venturing into the new and unusual. They like to experience new things and to understand how things work. The venturesome aspect of their personality enjoys trying the unknown just to see what it is like.

These are people who may never have had any interest in cooking but one day see an interesting dish and become intrigued and think, "I should try that," and off they go to cooking classes. Where does that come from? From possibility thinking and a curious personality.

Over the years in my work with people in one-on-one meeting environments, I have found almost everyone has at least some level of curiosity. We all wonder about some things, but some of us more than others.

What would it be like if you spent a few minutes for a few days in a row wondering what sorts of things interest you? You might produce a short list, but I can assure you, you will have a list of things that you have at least a mild interest in. If one of those items is especially interesting to you and you choose to explore it, you may find your curiosity and venturesome spirit awakens to a new and unique experience that ultimately produces enjoyment for you and others for the rest of your life.

THE RIPPLE EFFECT

There is another unique benefit that comes from spending time in your Personal Slice. It validates taking care of yourself. Everyone I have spoken with agrees that when they take some time for themselves, it helps them in every other part of their lives. The self-care concept is gaining speed in our society because people are learning that unless they take care of themselves, more than likely no one else will. To a large degree, self-care is just pausing to listen to your thoughts, body, and emotions. It means paying attention to the events in your day to make sure you don't get overwhelmed, overwrought, or overly absorbed in the ups and downs and emotional swings of daily life.

We lose this feeling, I believe, when we are focused on achieving in the Professional Slice and loving and caring in the Family Slice. To care for yourself, you don't have to take time away from another Slice—you simply must take the time needed to invest just enough to receive the benefit. Many have commented, and I believe it is true, that when you spend any amount of time in this Slice, you are just *better* in the other Slices, which suggests that your attitude changes in a positive way. Since you are doing something that makes you happy, fulfilled, or both, you reflect that feeling of happiness to the world and people around you. They notice and often respond in kind.

SLICE CASE STUDY: JACK

Jack had a career in sales with a well-known medical device company in New Jersey. He was good but not spectacular at his job. What he really wanted was to be inside the business in an operating position rather than outside selling the products. He liked the company and the products, and with the specialty in cardiac surgery medical devices, he had the opportunity to sit in the operating rooms of the hospital clients and see how the products helped save lives.

Jack and I crossed paths when he was finally given the chance to change his career path and his employer moved him into the product development division. In his new position, Jack reported to the senior vice president of product development, a person I had worked with for years, focusing on leadership development skills. Shortly after Jack joined the team, I had an opportunity to introduce myself to him and get a sense of how this new job might impact Jack and how he would function in the team going forward.

A Japanese American, Jack was in his late forties, married with two children, and living in a suburb in New Jersey. His wife of 20 years, Paula, was a stay-at-home mom. When Jack and I started working together, his daughter was in high school and his son was in junior high. His parents had emigrated from Japan to San Francisco, where they raised Jack (the middle child) and Jack's two brothers. All were raised to respect and honor their elders, to work hard, and to serve their community. His parents were very loving, and he was particularly close to his father, who owned a dry-cleaning business and worked hard. His mother was a devoted caregiver, doted on the three boys, and raised them to work around the house since they were young. As a result, Jack said that hard work was part of his identity and that he found it hard to stop working, even when appropriate.

I asked Jack how things were going as he entered this new division of the company, particularly because he had no real background in product development. Jack shared that while his first six years in the company had been very successful with biannual promotions and pay raises, his last two years had been extraordinarily bumpy and disappointing to him.

Two years ago, his boss thought he was ready to step up and run the sales team. Jack was a top producer, but certainly not *the* top producer. The promotion came as quite a surprise to the other salespeople, and they did not respond well to the announcement that Jack would be their new leader. Jack, being a believer that hard work and good intentions overcome any business obstacle, took on the challenge and was convinced he could win over the members of the team.

Without asking, I knew that things hadn't gone well. As Jack explained, the first few months were painful trying win over the support of the team. It turned out the leading producer waged a silent gossip campaign against Jack, motivated in part by his feeling that he had been unfairly passed over for the position. Jack had no knowledge of that at the time, but naturally when he did find out, he was upset.

On top of that, in Jack's first year in the leadership position, the team members missed their combined sales goals for the calendar year for the first time in over a decade. When Jack received a mediocre review accompanied with no pay increase, he knew that year two was do or die for him.

At this point, I asked if he had asked for help, given that he was dealing with a particularly challenging people problem on his team. His response was that you did not do that. Instead, he said, "You need to buckle down and see it through and find a way to make it work."

After six more months of stagnant sales and no improvement in team morale, Jack made the decision, for his family and his health, to pursue a better work-life balance. He approached his boss and requested a change. His boss responded by moving him laterally into the product development division, although some people believed it was a demotion of sorts.

When I asked how he felt about that, he said, "Right now, that is the least of my problems."

Sometimes our life's problems come in bunches, particularly if we have been ignoring or suffering from "blind spots" in our careers. I was starting to suspect that Jack may be one of those people when, over the next several weeks, we talked about the mounting challenges in his life.

It turned out that what people thought about his new position was the least of his worries. As Jack began to tell his tale, he paused to explain that he had been a worrier all his life. Back in grade school and all the way through college, he overthought and overworried about things that never occurred. Yet even though he realized after the fact that the anticipated calamity failed to materialize, he went right ahead and found something new to worry about. Whether it was a test, a project, or whatever, he worried himself sick over the possibility of failure each time.

The fact that he succeeded most of the time, and certainly did not fail, made no difference to his capacity to worry about the next challenge in front of him. When I asked why he didn't address that as he entered his career and family life, he shrugged and suggested, "It's just the way I am wired."

I suggested that we go back to this issue later. Clearly, he felt a comfort level with a consistently high level of self-imposed stress. Ultimately, for his own health, I felt that would have to be resolved and probably sooner rather than later.

Before we started working together, and he had just started in the sales leadership position, Jack's travel schedule increased dramatically. The reason he brought this up was because it did not sit well with his wife. As a sales representative, he had the East Coast as his territory for years—so when he did have to travel, it was for a day or just one overnight stay. When he became a sales leader, his travel often entailed being away from home for several days at a time and sometimes more depending on the month.

His wife had resented his travel because Jack wasn't home to help with the children and their school issues. In addition, she demonstrated a sudden and intense jealousy streak. She became convinced Jack was meeting women on the road while staying at various luxury hotels.

He assured her that there was nothing to worry about, and he adjusted his schedule by taking more red-eye flights home from the West Coast, often landing at 6 a.m. to appease her.

However, their relationship continued to worsen. On the weekends when the family was all together, his wife distanced herself from Jack. She would leave the house sometimes for the whole day by herself or with her daughter in an attempt at some kind of "payback" directed at Jack.

While beset by marriage worries, Jack was simultaneously trying to resolve the challenge of managing an unsupportive and disengaged work team. On top of everything else, he was concerned that his two children were going to suffer as the tension level in the house continued to grow.

And remember, Jack was a worrier by nature, who fretted over things even when there wasn't anything to worry about. Not surprisingly, the situation triggered anxiety and depression in Jack. His work had never been more stressful, and his home provided no respite.

All this motivated Jack to ask for a new work assignment. He hoped the move into the product development position would solve the work and family problems that were engulfing his life. And at first, it appeared that it might work out that way.

But according to Jack, while his relationship with his wife improved somewhat, it didn't go back to the place it used to be. Instead, it became something akin to a partnership rather than a marriage. His wife, Jack explained, was a very analytical person, whereas Jack was clearly a feeler and a big-picture thinker. These are differences that complement each other when at ease—but can create a perfect conflict situation when under stress. What most upset Jack was the fact that his wife had little to no interest in what he was feeling and going through. One night, while trying to explain to her the challenge he was having at work and why he was feeling scared about it, she cut him off in mid-sentence and said, "It's not that big a deal. You make mountains out of molehills." And she left the room.

At that point, Jack wasn't even angry about it—he felt mostly deflated and disillusioned by her and her comments. In his mind, it was a turning point, and he knew the marriage was in serious trouble.

As the saying by Hans Selye goes: "It's not stress that kills us; it is our reaction to it."

I asked Jack about his physical and mental health. Not surprisingly, neither was going well. He was on prescription anxiety medications, which he took primarily to fall asleep, as he was beginning to suffer from insomnia.

Jack explained that he always felt the stress in the form of stomach cramps, and they often were bad enough to stop him from eating. With his stress higher than ever, he was losing weight at an unhealthy rate, which made him even more distressed. Amazingly, Jack's demeanor and personality remained consistent, meaning he was the same pleasant, easygoing person in the office and with his children at home. While that might seem positive, what it meant is that no one was aware of the exceedingly difficult life he was living in this moment. He said it made him feel like he was alone in the middle of a crowd.

As I observed Jack, I noted that he was a "learn-it-all" kind of person. He was interested in new things. People were drawn to him in the office environment because he always responded to new ideas, with curious questions like "That sounds really interesting. Can you tell me more about that?"

So it was no surprise that Jack took to the Seven-Slice Method with the approach of a student. He studied it, asked questions, and had me outline it on the whiteboard in his office. He wanted to know every detail about each Slice, and he prepared questions about the different Slices in advance of our meetings.

When I had introduced the method to Jack, I explained that it provided a way to find harmony in our lives so that we could navigate our way through our stresses and pressures. But while Jack clearly needed to find more harmony, his motivation in embracing the method was unique to him. He loved it because it was new, different, and interesting. To Jack, the learning was the exciting part. If the method worked for him, well then, that would be a bonus! We all have our own motivations, and if they help us to get started, then it's all good!

Once he fully understood each Slice of his pie chart, he grappled with the questions that accompanied each Slice. Jack took this as a personal mission to get to the bottom of each Slice in his own life. He probed to answer the questions both on a practical level and on a deeper, more psychological level.

As I pointed out earlier, Jack felt things deeply. It was very normal for him to assign a feeling to almost everything that happened in his life. His approach to the Seven-Slice Method would be no different. First, Jack labored over the percentages in each Slice to make sure that he was completely honest with himself. Then he answered the questions in each Slice thoroughly and took pains to explain all the details regarding his answers and how he arrived at the percentages. When he finished answering the questions, he printed his answers out; they totaled over *40 pages*. The average number of pages I had seen from others prior to meeting Jack was seven.

When he measured his time percentage in each Slice, he decided to look at it from both today's percentages and what he thought it was 10 years ago so he could compare.

The percentages of time from 10 years ago looked like this:

- The Family Slice: 20 percent
- The Professional Slice: 70 percent
- The Personal Slice: 5 percent
- The Physical Slice: 0 percent
- The Intellectual Slice: 2 percent
- The Emotional Slice: 1 percent
- The Spiritual Slice: 2 percent

The percentages in the current timeline looked like this:

- The Family Slice: 20 percent
- The Professional Slice: 75 percent

- The Personal Slice: 0 percent
- The Physical Slice: 0 percent
- The Intellectual Slice: 0 percent
- The Emotional Slice: 0 percent
- The Spiritual Slice: 5 percent

Jack's immediate reaction was wonderment. How could he have let so many parts of his life just lie dormant for so long? He pointed out that his Spiritual Slice had only increased because his wife was deeply religious and insisted that they attend church services and the children attend Sunday school classes every week. Jack was raised in the United States as a Christian and attended church services with his family every week but admitted that was about the extent of it. He did not think he was getting much out of it because his heart was not in it.

I asked what he learned from his deep dive into the Slices. He responded that for the first time ever he thought about his life in terms of where it was years ago and where it is now. He said this motivated him to reflect on where he wanted his life to go in the future. He wanted to make a plan to make sure that 10 years from now he would have devoted sufficient time to each Slice that he would be whole again. Jack was taking a long view, which seemed to settle him down in the moment, a characteristic that I rarely found in clients and something I noted for future reference.

While taking the long view was great, the question Jack faced was, "What can I do now to reduce my anxiety so that I'm not overwhelmed as I start in my new role and with it, a new set of expectations?"

Jack decided to take a slightly different approach than most clients. He wanted to focus on the one thing he could change in one Slice of his life that would affect all the other Slices.

Why did this make sense for Jack? He explained that after analyzing his answers to the Slice questions, he realized he had to address his internal life first. He wanted to find out why he let himself slip into this emotionally precarious position. And why, throughout his life, had he ceded control over his life to others.

Jack plumbed each Slice to determine which Slice would present the best opportunity to teach him what he thought he needed to learn based on the state of his relationships with the people in his life at this moment in time.

An important note: Jack took this approach because he was very sure that he knew himself, and he wanted to change his life for the better due to his heightened sense of anxiety and stress. I share this with you as an example because you might find it helpful, but by no means is this a "one-size-fits-all" suggestion. For one thing, Jack's level of commitment was much greater than the average person's.

Here is how Jack thought his way through each Slice, given his circumstances:

- **The Family Slice.** Ten years ago, this Slice of his life was in good shape. He and his wife had two children together, and they were pursuing their mutually agreed goals of family, financial security, and a loving relationship. They were young, and their world was filled with hope and high expectations.

  Today was quite different. He felt uncomfortable in his marriage. And not only were both his children at boundary-pushing ages, but they had also picked up on the friction between their parents and had started to act distant toward their father.

- **The Professional Slice.** Ten years ago, this was a joyful part of Jack's life. He was energized at work, stimulated by all there was to learn, and inspired by the financial and developmental rewards. He looked forward to getting up in the morning and heading to the office. He had a large peer group that he enjoyed working with, and the people in the group would often socialize together with their wives. Many of them, like Jack, were starting to launch their careers and families, so they had a great deal in common. The pressure, of course, was much lower than what he later experienced. Climbing the ladder in the company back then was interesting and fun.

  Now the environment and his situation were much different. While he liked his new role, in some ways he was restarting his career, albeit with much more pressure and risk than 10 years ago. Though he was a positive guy, Jack self-assessed that he was "down"; and while his energy level was good, it wasn't where he would like it to be. The future, though potentially bright for him, seemed much more challenging compared with what it was 10 years ago. And unlike 10 years ago when he had a larger and more engaged peer group, now he felt very alone. Everything just felt heavy to him.

- **The Physical Slice.** Jack explained he was blessed with good genes, and for most of his life he was able to stay in shape just by eating right and going about his daily routines. Even now, despite what he'd put his body through, the constant stress had not snowballed into any serious heart or respiratory issues or any other major problem. His doctor advised him that his current health issues with insomnia would likely go away if he could address the stress. He suggested that Jack play the occasional client golf match and ride a bike with his children on weekends. Jack realized he did not have an active physical life, but he was fine with that as long as he remained healthy. Looking further ahead, he imagined he might take up skiing or hiking if his children wanted to, but probably not otherwise.

- **The Intellectual Slice.** Ten years ago, Jack was a "practical" reader of articles and books—he would read them if they had a direct impact on his work life. For example, he read several books about raising children when his kids were babies. Back then, to perform effectively as a salesperson to hospitals and surgical centers, he had to learn about medical devices and surgical procedures and processes. In addition, he had to discover who the decision-makers were before meeting with potential clients, so his research often included spending hours on LinkedIn and other sites.

  As the years went by and he became more familiar with the industry and his clients, he found he had to do less reading and research, which was a welcome development. Ten years ago, he was studying people more; today he studied how devices could make surgeries simpler and less expensive.

- **The Emotional Slice.** Ten years ago, Jack was a relatively happy guy. He tended to go with the flow and avoid conflict, which was sometimes a problem. He was and remained comfortable and at ease talking about his feelings. One of his strengths was his empathy in dealing with other people.

  He liked and enjoyed people who were comfortable coming to him to ask his opinion or to express an idea or feeling. He was much more engaged with friends and colleagues 10 years ago compared with today, and that greatly disappointed him. He said that he always thought of himself as the kind of person who put others and their needs above and before his own. Over time, that had changed, and he now found himself much more withdrawn and self-interested. Though his Family and Professional Slices were challenging, he felt it was no excuse for abandoning one of his core beliefs, which was to be connected with the important people around him. He felt strongly that he had to change this for him to feel good about himself again.

- **The Spiritual Slice.** Ten years ago, Jack said he was spiritual but not deeply religious. Raised in the Christian faith, he drifted away from attending church services after high school, but he continued to have faith in God. With the birth of his children, Jack started attending Sunday church services again, but he wasn't getting much out of it except for the occasional sermon message that stirred his feelings about his faith. He prayed, but not regularly; and this was another area he wanted to change because as he said he believed in the power of prayer. And again, he wondered why all this had changed so much in his life.

I reminded Jack he had left out one Slice in his very thorough review of the Slices: the Personal Slice. He explained that was deliberate, and he wanted now to share his plan for using the Seven-Slice Method to find his way back to a more peaceful, fulfilling life, and it revolved around the Personal Slice.

He prefaced his comments by saying he had selected this Slice because after some reflection, he realized that over the past decade he had slowly lost his own sense of himself. He decided that the Personal Slice was the one that he could pour the other Slices into and reclaim the person he knew he was and could be again with a little time and focused effort. As Jack summed up: "If I am not good for myself, I will never be good for anyone else."

So he laid out a simple plan to spend more time in his Personal Slice. Given that he felt he had lost his sense of self, he would start seeing a psychotherapist regularly, and this would be the foundational activity from which he would add other Slice activities (as was appropriate and practical) over the next year.

He wanted a therapist who was used to dealing with people like him and fit his profile so he would feel relaxed and could work quickly to get to the bottom of his issues. He was taking this on the same way he would take on a project at work; it felt comfortable for him, and he was energized to begin.

I asked why this approach made sense to him.

He said that there were going to be plenty of issues, particularly in his marriage, that would require him to really plan and think about how to deal with them directly—at which time, he would need his Physical, Emotional, and Spiritual Slices to help him cope with that process. By approaching his challenge in this way, he felt he had a better chance to find the harmony missing in his life. He said he believed that he would spend the time in four of the Slices, but by focusing on the Personal Slice at the start, he would be prepared to call on the other Slices for support when he needed them and would more likely use them and stay connected to them. Without this approach, he thought he would just slide back into his prior behaviors and ignore the other Slices when he did not need them.

On several levels, I thought this was brilliant. Not only did it motivate him to take action, but it allowed him to incorporate the other Slices as appropriate.

So how did this unique self-examination approach work out for Jack?

First, he realized that this was going to take time. As is frequently said, *Time takes time.* But Jack was very committed to getting to the bottom of the issues that were holding him back, and he was convinced that he needed to do this now or he would never do it. He felt that if he could discover why he did some of the things that created problems in his life, he would be more relaxed and more likely to invest in the other Slices of his life that he had all or mostly ignored.

Jack had an ambitious goal, and ultimately it took him two years to reach a point where he felt a sense of harmony. Sometimes things happen quickly, and other times we must wait for the process to unfold almost on its own.

During this period of self-examination and reflection, Jack was not dwelling on his issues every day. He moved forward deliberately, but not obsessively. After several months, Jack learned one key thing that changed the course of his development. Though it might not appear to be groundbreaking to you or me, it only matters to the person experiencing the insight. Through this process, Jack learned that he was clearly a "pleaser."

This was a bit of a wakeup call in that Jack thought it explained why he had become both anxious and resentful while navigating his family and professional responsibilities.

According to Jack, he demonstrated this behavior for as long as he could remember. He recounted many examples of how his desire to please others affected his decision-making because he literally put his own wishes aside and went with another person's decision since it meant that they would get along better.

In fact, he had been burying his own point of view for so long that he felt nervous about changing. He noted that over the past several years, his resentment had grown to the point where he now was feeling the pain of the people he was trying to please and who were actually causing him to suffer in his professional life in the company. His point of view took second to the views of everybody else. It just seemed easier to Jack to go along to get along and to clam up in meetings even when he thought things should be done in a different way. Over time, he resented it.

I said on more than one occasion: "Jack, you're a pretty smart guy. If you think it should be a different way, why not suggest it?" And he'd make up excuses—legitimate, but still excuses. This extended to his family life—Jack's instinct was to do what everyone else wanted rather than pushing for compromise. So part of what we worked on was developing skills to help him disagree with someone respectfully and not to surrender his own voice.

The rest of Jack's story was a testament to his commitment and courage to make his life better. The details are voluminous, and I was fortunate to observe Jack's progress over the next several years. He devoted time to his Personal Slice in order to first discover what was his responsibility and then to determine how he would move forward in a positive way by using the other Slices of his life to enhance and quicken the process. Once there, he approached the other six Slices in a process that made sense for Jack. This made a big difference especially to his Family and Professional Slices:

- **The Family Slice updated.** He approached his wife and explained that he realized that he was not happy with the way things were and suggested he had not been fair because he was acting out an appeasement model instead of being totally honest with himself and her. This led them to seek couples therapy together, which went OK but not great, and they ultimately stopped going after a year. His wife wanted things to stay the same, but Jack needed the relationship to grow and become more of a loving marriage instead of a partnership. They reached a stalemate at that point.

- **The Professional Slice updated.** Jack strived to be less of a pleaser and more of an active agent in his own life. He began to ask more direct questions about his role in the company and to state what he preferred to see happen rather than waiting for his superiors to seek him out.

  Though it was enormously challenging for him, he approached his boss and asked what the prospects were for two or more promotions over the next several years. Up until then, Jack had always waited for promotions or pay raises. His boss was quite comfortable with the question and the subsequent conversation. His message was a definitive "maybe" based on Jack's ability to improve two or three executive skills over the next several years.

The benefit for Jack was twofold: First, obtaining the information allowed him to better assess his next steps. Second, and more important, Jack had taken a bold step in standing up for himself, and it led to a constructive discussion. Moreover, Jack's boss had taken no offense by his direct approach. This was enlightening to Jack, because he realized that advocating for himself was a good thing and not a punishable offense. He felt a burden had been lifted off his shoulders.

With this newfound assurance, Jack felt it was time to start addressing how to get his other Slices in place and where he might benefit from that time investment.

He thought the Physical Slice would be the best next step. Jack had never needed much exercise to stay in shape, fortunately, but he wanted to find a physical activity that he did not have to do alone. He decided to take a 25-minute walk around his suburban neighborhood every morning before breakfast with his black Lab in tow. The family dog was more for the children, so this exercise gave him and the dog some time together. Jack started to enjoy the walks and found that they helped him to start the day with a positive feeling. In addition, the walks gave him a chance to start thinking about his Spiritual Slice.

He said it just sort of crept up on him, but after a couple of weeks, Jack recognized that he really liked the silence in those early morning walks together. It was still too early for traffic, school buses, and people to disturb the calm. In the quiet, Jack found himself starting to pray again, although he wasn't sure if it was really praying or having a conversation. He asked questions and sought guidance and faith from a higher power to get through the day. He said it felt like a one-way conversation, but he started to look forward to it. He decided he wanted to reconnect his relationship with God, and just that idea gave him a calm sense of comfort. He claimed it was the first time in his life he felt this while praying.

All his work that he was doing in his Personal Slice produced yet another benefit: he became interested in the subject of personal self-development, and that ignited his Intellectual Slice.

He began reading several books on psychology and personal development, including business books on leadership and management, from which he thought he would greatly benefit. This was quite a change for him, as he admitted that he had not finished reading a single book in the last 15 years. Jack had a genuine thirst for knowledge, and once it was ignited, he began to read every day—not out of need, but out of want. He looked forward to it, and he always made time at the end of the evening to read at least a chapter of whatever book he was reading at the time.

As we mentioned before, the Personal Slice is tied to freedom. Rather than pleasing others, Jack found something just for him. He said it was "fun." Relatively speaking, this is an example of going from zero to 60 seconds in no time flat!

It did dawn on Jack that his Personal Slice had incorporated his Emotional Slice quite seamlessly and unintentionally, but with very satisfying results. In fact, his Emotional Slice was also showing up in his Intellectual Slice as he pursued the subjects of psychology and self-improvement. He shared another insight that came out of his experience with self-discovery. On a personal level, he always thought of himself as being superficial and interested in just what was in front of him. He never saw himself as intellectually curious or interested in large subjects that impacted the world. But this whole experience had changed his perspective on himself. He now enjoyed the learning process and the time it took to think about complicated subjects in order to find the right answer or the path forward for his life.

You might be wondering how Jack's life evolved during this period. After several more years, Jack and his wife decided that they had grown too far apart, and they divorced amicably without causing too much disruption to their children's lives. Jack bought a house near the neighborhood where the kids grew up, and he provided well for his ex-wife. The first couple of years were rocky with the kids visiting and school issues, but today the kids are successfully in college, and Jack has remarried and looks and sounds delightfully happy.

The medical device company that he worked for was acquired, and due to his length of service there, Jack was able to leave with a comfortable severance package. That allowed him to take some time to find a job that would make sense for him. He managed to secure a senior-level position in business development with a smaller medical device company. He finds his role to be invigorating, and he is well respected in the new company.

Through his experience going from a very low period of his life to a much healthier place, Jack realized the importance of devoting time and activities to the five other Slices of his life. It is not unusual for him to email me a book or article that he found interesting and relates to the work I do. We still get together every few months. His desire for personal discovery remains strong, and he has achieved a sincere and mature happiness that manifests by living with joy, commitment, and curiosity.

CHAPTER SUMMARY

If you're not sure where to start with the Personal Slice, ask yourself, "What am I interested in today?"

Not yesterday, not when you were a kid, but *today*! The big thing with the Personal Slice is that it's all about the moment. It's not about the future or the past. It's about today, now, what you would like to do that's both relaxing and fulfilling just for you. Try exploring what you are interested in rather than pursuing something popular. If I gave you this afternoon to do exactly what you wanted to do, what would you do? Some people need to stop and think about that. That's a Personal Slice activity in itself—thinking of what would benefit you today.

THE PHYSICAL SLICE

Many of us take our bodies for granted due to our overcrowded and busy schedules. Yet the state of our body's health has a direct impact on every other aspect of our lives. After all, your body is the vehicle that carries you in each Slice of your life. It's critical that we take care of ourselves.

When we talk about your Physical Slice, we're talking about everything that impacts your physical body—exercise, diet, sleep, medical care, and a variety of other factors that contribute to how your body functions throughout your life.

Everyone deals with short-term health issues, such as sprains, cuts, colds, coughs, etc. Many of us, particularly as we age, develop chronic conditions that require ongoing treatments and/or lifestyle changes.

In any case, your body is a living thing that requires maintenance to perform at its best.

TAKING STOCK OF YOUR PHYSICAL SLICE

Understandably, people get a little sensitive about this Slice. How you take care of yourself is very personal. The thing to focus on in this Slice isn't the judgment of others or what you think you're doing wrong, but rather, "What can I do to improve how I feel and potentially touch this Slice more on a regular basis?"

When working with clients, I'll ask them generally, "So physically, how are you doing?"

The answers run the gamut, from "Well, I've got high blood pressure—my doc told me I should go on medication, but I haven't done it yet," to "I've gained some weight recently that I'm not happy about," to "I don't get enough sleep—and when I do it's not great," to "I used to exercise a lot, but now I just don't have time"—and everything in between. Most people have something physically going on that they wish they could improve.

I also ask clients: "How's your energy level? Do you have enough energy to tackle every day?"

The energy question is important—after all, leadership and management require a certain amount of energy. If you're always feeling drained and low on energy, your appearance will likely reflect your fatigue. Your team and colleagues undoubtedly will notice you look tired, and it will impact how they interact with you.

Not to browbeat anyone, but you need to do something to manage your physical life. No one's figured out how to stop the aging process yet. Whether you like it or not, your body will decay over time. The average person's muscle mass decreases 3–8 percent per year every year after 30 without exercise.[1] Hence you see people in their seventies who are much smaller than they were in their fifties. Their muscles are shrinking. That should be a good motivator to anyone to do something to ease the aging process.

Apart from the long-term issues attendant to aging, the state of your physical body influences how you feel right now—and how you feel can play a big role in managing your stress.

THE ROLE OF STRESS IN OUR PHYSICAL SLICE

Stress is an unavoidable part of life. In the short term, it provides a heightened feeling of alertness that can be helpful in getting us to meet a deadline or to perform at our best.

However, many professionals live under constant pressure and are busy all the time. This impacts how they feel physically. And over time, constant stress can take a big toll on their bodies and how they function.

To repeat the adage from Selye from Chapter 5: "It's not stress that kills us; it is our reaction to it."

Stress isn't just "all in your head." When you perceive any kind of a threat—whether it's a bear lumbering out of the bushes toward your campsite or an impending high-stakes deadline, your body has a stress response.

As the Mayo Clinic staff explains, when you feel threatened, here's how your body responds:

> Your hypothalamus, a tiny region at your brain's base, sets off an alarm system in your body. Through a combination of nerve and hormonal signals, this system prompts your adrenal glands, located atop your kidneys, to release a surge of hormones, including adrenaline and cortisol.
>
> Adrenaline increases your heart rate, elevates your blood pressure, and boosts energy supplies.
>
> Cortisol, the primary stress hormone, curbs functions that would be nonessential or detrimental in a fight-or-flight situation. It alters immune system responses and suppresses the digestive system, the reproductive system and growth processes. This complex natural alarm system also communicates with the brain regions that control mood, motivation and fear.[2]

In other words, you don't just "feel" stressed. Your body, in its attempt to protect you, is physically reacting. And over time, those physical reactions have consequences.

Prolonged periods of stress can result in many types of physical and mental health issues. Some of the most common are pain, spasms, muscle tightness, and soreness in our joints. Many people feel the effect of stress in the "tension triangle," consisting of their head, jaw, and shoulders. A sense of tightness, pain, or fatigue in that area tells us we are under pressure. As many medical experts assert again and again, we need to "listen" to our bodies, sense when we're under too much stress, and take steps to relax and feel better.[3]

Furthermore, stress can prompt flare-ups of arthritis and other symptoms.[4] The primary reason for this is because stress lowers our threshold for pain endurance. In other words, not only does stress cause issues—it can also impact our ability to deal with the issues they cause. Stress also directly impacts our immune system, which creates the condition for chronic lung infections and lowers our ability to fight off disease. In addition, a lowered immune system leaves us vulnerable to autoimmune conditions like lupus that reduce our ability to function at high levels.[5, 6]

We are all familiar with the damage unchecked stress can cause to our heart and lungs. Cortisol, the stress hormone mentioned above, can contribute to high blood pressure, cardiovascular disease, heart disease, and asthma.[7] How many of us have experienced a racing heart rate when the pressure runs very high? Sometimes, it can get a little scary.

Our digestive system can be another victim of unmanaged stress. Digestive issues affect many people and often lead to chronic conditions with complex and hard-to-manage symptoms.[8]

Of course, if you have persistent pain symptoms that you suspect are caused by stress, it's always a good idea to check in with your doctor to rule out other conditions. However, if stress is clearly the main culprit, we need to listen to what our bodies are telling us. It's not as simple as the pain being "all in your head." The symptoms are signaling a problem that we need to find and address

As people grow older, their Physical Slice can become quite painful. Many people suffer incredible challenges, such as arthritis of the spine or the knees. Even moving around can become a challenge. To ignore this Slice obviously creates more stress in other Slices. At a young age, it's best to start taking care of yourself to give yourself the best chance of avoiding ill-health and reaping the many benefits that the Physical Slice can provide, including improved emotional and mental health.

It's important to be aware of the mind-body connection. For example, most people who have open-heart surgery are encouraged by their medical professionals to seek psychotherapy so that the recovery sticks and they don't become depressed.[9] The mind and the body work together in many ways.

Attending to the Physical Slice, of course, isn't a cure-all. When the symptoms scream loudest and you start to talk with someone about the situation, invariably the problem lies in one of the other Slices of your life.

The point being that while our bodies receive stress physically, the stress can originate from worry, financial concerns, concerns about the health of other family members, loss of employment, and on and on. But wherever the origin, your body takes the shot. When people are miserable at their jobs, the body can only handle the intense stress for a maximum of 18 months in a row before it starts to break down. We often warn executive teams working under stress that they need to find a pressure valve release so they don't burn themselves out. Everyone talks about emotional burnout—but the physical body burns out too. You might recall the problem of accumulation that we discussed in Chapter 1. You already have problems—and if you don't take care of your body, your body will introduce more problems.

That is why it is important to invest in our other Slices, so we can save our physical body from too much wear and tear where we can.

OVERCOMING RESISTANCE

It's unlikely that the core message of this chapter is new to you. Everyone knows that eating well, exercising, and staying on top of other health needs is good for you. Managing our weight, keeping muscles firm, and following a healthy diet all makes sense to everyone.

Yet many people still neglect their Physical Slice, rationalizing that they must sacrifice it in the service of work or family.

The work environment is often part of the problem. Sure, some workplaces—such as those in Silicon Valley—design their offices and campuses to include gyms and walking paths, as well as encourage employees to utilize exercise bicycles in the office or treadmills that enable them to walk and work at the same time.

Most companies, however, do not have those environments. Some new office buildings include a gym for their employees to join—but while wellness at work is growing, it's not ingrained in most company cultures. Most employers still consider exercise and wellness to be their employees' responsibility. And many workplaces require you to sit for long periods of time.

Moreover, attending to the Physical Slice can be a tall order if you struggle with various health issues. "I'm already dealing with this and that, and now you want me to do more?"

Other common refrains are "I'm just lazy" and "I don't like exercise." I've noticed that when people's only exposure to the Physical Slice was forced (for example, gym class in school or a sport their parents forced them to play), they tend to struggle finding a physical regimen that they can stick to. Remember that you can interact with this Slice on your own terms. For some people, yoga is perfect because it combines their Physical Slice with their Spiritual Slice. For others, reducing the amount of sugar they consume daily makes a big difference in how they feel emotionally or physically. Some people find an extreme sport matches their intense personality. Others like to go for regular walks or jogs with a friend because it combines the physical with the social and makes them forget that they're exercising.

Maybe you think you don't have time to exercise or take care of your health beyond the bare minimum. If so, try making a list of everything you do in a day. Most likely you'll find you often make time for other things, but don't prioritize physical activity or self-care. There are ways to schedule short breaks in a day to do something that has to be done. We all do it when we must.

Once again, it is about making a decision about something we believe is important. What if spending 10 minutes a day walking fast could save you a struggle with weight or high blood pressure later in your life? Would you do it?

This gets to one of the other reasons why you might resist living in the Physical Slice regularly. Everything today is immediate. But the Physical Slice requires patience and the ability to delay gratification. One 10-minute walk is not going to lower your blood pressure the next day. Nor are you going to drop those 10 pesky pounds after one jogging session.

The diet industry banks on this, and every five years or so there comes along another newly minted diet that claims to help you lose tens of pounds easily and in no time at all! Oh, if it were that simple. While people need to make their own choices, I urge you to choose a diet and fitness regimen that you can stick to rather than one that's advertised as a quick fix.

MORE PHYSICAL

There are myriad ways to exercise, and I'm always amazed by how creative some are. Exercise can be as simple as a regular walk or jog, or as involved as racquet sports, basketball, baseball, hockey, skating, swimming, golf, gym workouts, skiing, hiking, mountain climbing, or snowshoeing, and let's not forget the personal trainer programs. Personal training is often a good fit for those that need a schedule and another person to keep them on track and responsible to the commitment. Whatever works for you is the one that you should choose.

THE BENEFITS OF SPENDING MORE TIME IN YOUR PHYSICAL SLICE

Since we can all agree there are benefits to paying attention to our physical well-being, let's talk about how you can integrate the Physical Slice into your go-go-go, high-stress life.

In the world of behavioral management, there is an axiom that goes something like this: *If you want to change behavior in the short term, use a reward as the motivator. If you want to change behavior for the long term, use consequences as the motivator.* Just like the other Slices, time is the enemy of the Physical Slice. It takes time to exercise and change the blood flow in our bodies. However, the benefits are immense.

Making the effort to take care of your physical body each day through dieting, exercising, and getting appropriate medical care can bring short- and long-term benefits. The daily feeling of doing something positive, at the very least, improves your attitude and can get the ball rolling toward a sustained commitment.

There are two other benefits that can come out of this physical effort. First, you gain a sense of confidence as you get past the beginning of your program and continue in a disciplined manner. Second, the sense of accomplishing something that you previously thought was unachievable gives you a feeling of being more in control of a part of your life that really matters. Both feelings are by-products of your effort and contribute to improving your self-esteem.

Regular physical activity builds heart and lung capacity, lowers blood pressure, reduces weight gain, and has a positive impact on managing diabetes.[10] Getting your heart rate up to 140 beats per minute for 20 minutes a few times a week recharges your brain with a fresh dose of new blood flow that has the benefit of lifting your spirits and attitude.[11] From personal experience, exercise provides a refreshing break in the day and produces a healthy perspective on whatever else is happening that day.

Perhaps the single best benefit from taking some time and investing in your physical life is that it almost immediately reduces the stress you're feeling. The movement of your body just seems to allow your thoughts to move away from the problem and into the process that your body is going through.

SLICE CASE STUDY: KATHLEEN

Kathleen was a brilliant engineer and lawyer. She had worked for a life sciences company for years when she was recruited to become a partner in a boutique engineering consulting firm that specialized in the energy sector. She was in her early forties, had never married but had many relationships over the years, and was close with her family of origin. She often took her parents on family vacations to the Caribbean islands, and she doted on her niece who often spent weekends with Kathleen at her home in Chicago. She was highly active in women's business groups in Chicago and was a sought-after speaker due to her combined engineering and legal expertise. She was physically active and could be described as a work hard/play hard kind of person.

We met after she was recruited as a partner into the firm of one of my clients. The focus of my work at the firm was developing the leadership skills of the partners who ran the firm. I had been working with the founder of the firm, Marshall, for over a decade, and I understood him, the partnership, and the culture of the firm fairly well. When Kathleen joined the firm, Marshall suggested that I could help onboard her into the firm and quickly settle her into the flow of the firm and its work.

Kathleen and I hit it off right away. She had never worked with someone like me, but she eagerly participated in our sessions. Her background and strengths made her an outstanding asset for the firm because she was so technically strong and could produce amazing amounts of work in short periods of time. She grasped the work quickly, understood what was important, focused on the execution, and did it twice as fast as a peer and without errors.

However, her best traits, she explained, could also be a source of tension at work. Sometimes people resented her style, accusing her of being dismissive toward those who could not "keep up." I pointed out that many people have this experience and that the issue can be dealt with through effective communication and consensus building with colleagues and within executive teams.

She also had an additional challenge in that this was a partnership of 11 partners, and there tended to be more of an emphasis on consensus. Kathleen previously worked in corporate environments where there was a more structured sense of hierarchy in decision-making and where consensus building was less valued. She would have to adjust.

My role in working with Kathleen was to advise her about the firm's cultural issues, help her to adapt and fit into the firm fairly quickly, and coach specific executive skills that would help her carry out her leadership and management responsibilities.

Again, Kathleen was an eager learner and made good progress. The general perception was that after an adjustment period, she overcame the early bumps in the road and fit in nicely with the partnership team. We continued to meet for several more months and then agreed to reduce our meeting schedule—after all, she was extremely busy, and she needed to focus on the business client relationships.

About a year or so later, I received a call from the managing partner, Marshall, asking, "Is there something going on with Kathleen I should know about?"

I couldn't give him an answer; though Kathleen and I were supposed to be meeting once a month, we hadn't met in several months due to the higher-priority client urgencies.

Marshall called because while Kathleen's performance continued to be stellar with the client work, her partner behavior had slipped. He was getting feedback that indicated she was becoming withdrawn, rude at times, and intolerant with underperformers. In department meetings, if Kathleen disagreed with one of her boss's suggestions, she sometimes asked an awkward and uncomfortable question out loud, which would embarrass her boss as well as the other people in the room. It wasn't that she was asking bad questions—but they were the questions that should have been asked "offline," and not in a public setting. In the past, when she'd been more comfortable and relaxed, she acted appropriately and sought out the boss and asked the tough questions one-on-one (which her boss welcomed).

Due to her level of upset and stress, however, she temporarily lost a level of self-awareness. That happens to many people—you just don't see things as clearly when you're under great stress.

We had discussed these things at her entry point in the firm now almost two years ago. I asked Marshall if he had approached her about her change in behavior. He had and said she responded in a very pleasant manner and indicated she would work on it. However, Marshall said she did not seem to take the issue very seriously and was more focused on other priorities in the firm.

That was a problem—three of the partners had reported their frustration with her behavior, but she wasn't taking it seriously. Given the urgency, he asked us to pick up our sessions and meet more frequently.

In my work with client behavioral challenges, I have found one common variable: there is always a *why* behind the *what*. There is always a reason that can explain the unexplainable. Whatever the outlandish behavior might be, it is a certainty that behavior is solving another problem that is real to that person. And though the behavior clearly is creating new problems for that person, there is always another problem being solved that is a higher priority.

It was on that note that I went to meet with Kathleen at our scheduled meeting session. She greeted me warmly but with a bit of a more subdued demeanor than the last time we had met. We spoke about her work and the pressures that she was dealing with, but she indicated that it was really "fine" and it was under control.

I continued to ask business-oriented questions and then slowly turned toward asking more people-oriented questions about her partners at the firm, particularly their concern that she was demonstrating "sharp elbow" behavior. The shift was noticeable—Kathleen became testy, and her body language indicated that she was not in agreement with the feedback.

She explained her side of things. If there was disagreement with an individual, she pointed out, then it was certainly not entirely Kathleen's fault or sole responsibility. I agreed with her at this point and suggested that in most disagreements, there is a level of shared responsibility between the parties. She then sat back for a moment and said something that I hear from time to time in these situations.

"It's just not fair . . ." she said. She let that statement sit in the silence for a moment. I didn't push.

After a moment, she revealed the underlying tension in her life. Several months ago, she explained, during a routine examination with her medical doctor, tests revealed that her breast cancer, which had been in remission for four years, had returned. The diagnosis brought back painful memories of the original diagnosis and the ensuing treatment that included chemo, radiation, and surgery.

At that time, she had family support and the flexibility to balance her work schedule with her medical treatments and health needs. Her employer was supportive, and the experience, though frightening at times, ended well and successfully.

Due to her great health following the treatments, she felt confident in leaving a relatively safe corporate environment to take on the much more personal and riskier environment of a partnership. Having more control with potentially greater financial rewards appealed to her—and again, her health had improved, so why not?

With this latest diagnosis, however, she was very anxious that she had made the wrong call. She needed support and safety—but even after two years, she was still considered the "new" partner. Facing such a great medical challenge on what she perceived to be thin ice in her work environment concerned her.

Mortality is its own separate subject. But when it's your mortality at stake, the process can often be very lonely and scary. Kathleen was clearly in that place and as a result was not sure exactly how to handle this situation in her life.

Over the next several weeks, we had several discussions and mapped out a plan. Along the way she shared her health condition with Marshall, who agreed to keep this news confidential until she had a clearer understanding of the length of the treatments and how debilitating they may or may not become over the next six months or so.

Marshall was gracious and said the firm would be happy to support her, but the partners would just need advance notice so as to provide the staffing that might be required if she had to miss meaningful time from the office.

While this helped, Kathleen's stress level remained quite high due to the uncertainty of her situation. There was also another element—her family's health had taken a turn at this time, as well. Her father had recently suffered a fall and was now at home looking at potential surgery to replace his hip. Her mother was unable to shoulder the entire burden, so Kathleen was helping on the weekends and paying for a nurse to come in part-time during the week to provide some assistance until the surgery could be scheduled.

Clearly, Kathleen was dealing with an extreme situation in her life and was rightfully frightened. With all this swirling around her, I asked what frightened her the most. She rambled at first in her response but finally articulated her answer: though her medical doctors encouraged her to believe that they knew how to handle the return of the cancer and that her chance of survival was excellent, she had her doubts.

She wasn't sure of her body's ability to survive another attack of this kind. In addition to the cancer, she had dealt with a number of health issues in her life. Her immune system had been compromised years ago, prior to the first occurrence of cancer, and her body was susceptible to lung infection. That predisposition had made dealing with the cancer the first time especially difficult.

Fear dominated her life. Dejectedly, she shared that her chemo treatment would start the next week. She dreaded it. She knew that a positive attitude would serve her much better, but she was at a loss about how to get there.

Kathleen's Seven-Slice Plan

This was when I introduced the Seven-Slice Method to her. She was willing to try anything, but worried about finding the time. Together we did our best to streamline the process.

As you might imagine, her Family and Professional Slices took up most of her time, especially considering her devotion to her parents and niece. She took her time going through the rest of the Seven-Slice Method questions. We all have unique lives, and it is always interesting for me to learn how individual people will have a slightly different take on how they live in their Seven Slices.

In Kathleen's case, she saw her Slices carved up this way:

The Personal, Intellectual, and Spiritual Slices were combined and comprised around 15 percent of her time. She explained that she enjoyed reading about eclectic subjects. While she occasionally read about subjects dealing with her Professional Slice, primarily she pursued subjects that interested her personally. In particular, she was interested in the spiritual world. She read a great deal on science and religion to determine how she saw herself within the perspective of the universe, what the meaning of her life was here, and what lay beyond her physical life on earth. It was a subject that she had been reading about since she was in high school.

Though she attended church services occasionally, she considered herself more spiritual than religious. During her first bout with cancer five years ago, she reconnected with her church and spent more time attending services and praying. She still spent time in prayer but had drifted away from a consistent commitment.

The Emotional Slice was sporadic for her, she explained, and she couldn't put a percentage on it. During her cancer treatment, doctors recommended she find a therapist to talk with during the treatments. She had taken advantage of that during that trying period and found it extremely helpful at times. When she returned to good health, she touched base with her therapist occasionally when she felt the need. She said she would probably reengage with her therapist once the new treatments started.

Just taking the time to answer the questions in the Physical Slice gave her pause. Technically, she spent a lot of time in her Physical Slice. She followed her doctor's orders, attended treatments, and made sure she took her medicines as prescribed.

However, while her body had been through a lot over the past several years, she had spent no time trying to grow physically stronger. Her focus was staying alive. This was a disappointing revelation to her. She didn't even engage in simple physical activities, such as going for a regular walk.

What I found so interesting in Kathleen's profile was that whereas most of us can adjust and improve our stress levels by investing more time in neglected Slices, her solution was the opposite. For her to find more harmony, it appeared that she needed to find a way to invest even more in her Physical Slice. But how could she do that when she was restarting cancer treatments in a few days?

Given Kathleen's penchant for solving problems in most parts of her life, she approached this issue with intelligence and confidence. She set up an action plan and committed herself to see it through with optimism and persistence.

She met with her medical team to learn what other patients had been able to do physically while going through the rigors of chemo and radiation treatments. She learned that the answer varied from person to person. In her case, the team suggested that given that her physical health outside of the cancer was good, she could embark on a mild exercise program if she chose to. She was referred to a physical therapist within the medical practice, and together they determined what she could handle and how she could fit it into the rest of her complicated life. They initially kept it simple. Kathleen settled on walking for 15 minutes at a casual pace, two times per week. Over time if she felt confident and strong enough, she could increase the frequency.

Over the next several months, Kathleen made small steps with her time in her Physical Slice, while she was undergoing cancer treatments. As she admitted, initially the walks made little difference in her physical life, but the time spent walking was giving her hope that she would survive this health scare.

As for the office, she was able to keep up with most of her workload by working from home while she was in treatment. The partnership was supportive, and she was provided the flexibility she needed without any threat of losing stature in the firm, which was her initial concern.

After a little over a year, the treatments were completed, and she had recovered her strength. The process had given her a new perspective. She still had some anxiety (she had to wait five years before she'd be certain she was in the clear); however, with the rest of her life back in a regular cadence of activities and good health, she made a renewed commitment to the Physical Slice.

With the treatments behind her, Kathleen took control of her physical life in short order. She hired a personal trainer and began a regular twice-a-week workout in the early mornings near where she lived. She felt she needed the trainer; otherwise she would sleep in on those early mornings in the cold weather. She began to lose a little weight and felt her body getting stronger. She felt energized and healthier. She maintained the commitment and did not increase or decrease the frequency of her workouts. Ultimately, she decided to make the workouts part of her life, a habit rather than "a thing to do" for a while and then slow down or stop entirely.

It is important to note that as she began and continued this process, all the challenges outside of her health continued. She still had plenty to be stressed about around her family issues, work challenges in the partnership, and general life stresses that we all deal with every day. What made a difference was her commitment to spending consistent time in her Physical Slice and the positive motivation that developed within her.

Her medical team and her therapist reminded her that the key to maintaining her health was for her to focus on keeping a positive attitude. They both shared with her the data on the impact of positive thoughts on the human body and, conversely, the damage negative thoughts can cause. Kathleen shared with me that she had always struggled with pessimism. She received feedback along these lines in her professional life. Her family noticed it too and would talk to her about her gloominess when it got a little out of control.

Kathleen believed her renewed commitment to her Physical Slice had altered this habit in her and was more effective than simply trying to remind herself to think positive thoughts. Her personal trainer, as luck would have it, was an extremely positive person who was wildly encouraging to Kathleen and her progress.

This example where the stress and the solution to the stress were in one Slice demonstrates how by pausing to reflect, we can sometimes find the remedy to our stress within ourselves—and find it quickly. That makes all the difference.

CHAPTER SUMMARY

There are many ways to take better care of yourself. And by taking care of yourself, your Physical Slice can deliver many benefits to the rest of your Slices. In terms of managing your life successfully, having a healthy body makes the process much easier. As the saying goes: *If you have your health, you can solve any problem. If you don't, it makes it much more difficult.*

If you're looking for somewhere to start, ask yourself: "How do I feel about my body? What would have to change for me to feel good, or better? Are any of those changes under my control?"

There isn't a whole lot we can do about the set of genes we were born with, but all of us can focus on controlling the things we can control. How you take care of your physical health is in your hands.

THE INTELLECTUAL SLICE

You don't have to be an intellectual to have an active Intellectual Slice in your life. The Intellectual Slice is simply the part of your life where your curiosity lies—what you find interesting and the things you want to know more about.

There are many benefits to being curious and developing your interests.[1] I have worked with people who developed this part of their lives more and grew in a variety of ways. I suppose the easiest way to understand how to spend time in this Slice is to remember that old adage, *Be a learn-it-all, not a know-it-all*. Words to live by, but also the starting point to find a motivation to invest some time in this enriching area of your life.

EVALUATING YOUR INTELLECTUAL SLICE

The good news is that your Intellectual Slice isn't graded. It isn't even pass/fail. You don't have to go back to school (although some people do! I've had many clients who are driven to earn their master's or PhD in a subject they're passionate about). Some people touch this Slice by reading for a few minutes every night or by joining book clubs. Others listen to podcasts on nonwork-related subjects during their work commute. I've had other clients commit to writing and publishing an article in an industry publication.

Many people combine their Intellectual Slice with other Slices. For instance, you might pursue continuing education through your work (there-fore touching your Professional and Intellectual Slices). You might say, "I've always wanted to pick up woodworking." In that case, you're touching your Personal Slice since it's a personal interest, as well as your Intellectual since it involves learning. The same thing applies if you want to learn how to ski or do some other sport—there's a Physical Slice component *and* an Intellectual Slice component. Some of my clients have attended educational spiritual retreats, where they can attend their Spiritual Slice as well as their Intellectual.

Similarly, the length of time you spend in this Slice doesn't matter, as long as you spend time there consistently—a few times a week, once a week, once a month, whatever.

How can you tell if you're already attending this Slice? Ask yourself: "Am I learning something new regularly? And most importantly, does that learning experience provide me with a sense of renewal and refreshment?"

Feeling energized by how you spend your Intellectual Slice time is the key. Some people assume they have this Slice spoken for because they attend many continuing education workshops and receive training for their job. It's possible. But if the experience feels obligatory or draining, then it's not truly serving your Intellectual Slice.

Remember, the Intellectual Slice, like your Personal, Physical, Emotional, and Spiritual Slices, is there to help you disperse and manage stress. Therefore, when evaluating and taking stock of this Slice, don't worry about what you do or the amount of time doing it—instead, focus on how the activity makes you feel. The goal is to become more relaxed and refreshed.

When some people hear about the Intellectual Slice, they can immediately make a list of all the things they would like to learn and pursue. For others, it's not that easy. Many people lose touch with this Slice because they cede their intellectual interests to serving their Family and Professional Slices. My clients often tell me, "I know I haven't been spending any percentage of my time in this Slice, but I don't know where to start. I don't really have any interests." If you identify with that statement, it's essential to reconnect with your curiosity.

CURIOSITY

When we talk about curiosity, we're talking about "the desire to know." Curiosity is just something that you're interested in, regardless of whether it's a popular subject or activity or it's something that's out of the ordinary.

Curiosity is the driving force that has sparked almost everything of significance that has been built, discovered, or created, from discovering the world was not flat, to achieving space travel, to discovering and harnessing electricity, to inventing airplanes, and a million other things. Often, it is your curiosity that unlocks your potential to exceed your own expectations. Curiosity is that natural sense you have when you see something being done by someone else and you wonder, "How does that work?" and "Maybe I can do that, too." Curiosity frequently is the driving force behind taking on a difficult experiment in science, starting a new club in the school, or achieving a sports award on a team or in an individual sport.

As you grow older, your professional life requires a level of curiosity just to keep up. It starts in school when you are asked to study many different (and new to you) subjects and achieve excellence in each. Depending on what career path you choose, you may also enter college, graduate school, or vocational school. As you make choices regarding your education and career path, you likely are pursuing your curiosity (albeit out of necessity).

Oftentimes, people choose career paths that inspire them, and that inspiration can lead to breakthroughs for the benefit of our society. This happens in every field, from the arts to the sciences. The pharmaceutical industry, for example, rewards curious researchers and scientists who pursue solutions to the many illnesses where the cures are still unknown. Silicon Valley as well as the rest of the technology sector is filled with people who are driven by curiosity and creativity. Who could have imagined that we would have apps for smartphones, teleconferencing, privatized space travel, or self-driving cars a few years ago? We're in an age of almost unbridled curiosity.

In the face of all this achievement, your curiosity may seem insignificant to you. Don't be dissuaded. Your curiosity still matters, regardless of how much or how little it impacts the state of humanity. What's important is how your curiosity impacts your life.

HOW FOLLOWING YOUR CURIOSITY BENEFITS YOU

Your Intellectual Slice is driven by your interests. And when you follow your interests, two things happen.

First, your own level of energy changes for the better. Learning something new—particularly something new that you *want* to learn—is stimulating. Your brain, which is always running, now has a different flow of energy being produced.[2] Your enthusiasm and sense of accomplishment improve. That has a ripple effect—when people feel that they're progressing and improving, they're more likely to feel happiness. And as we all know, when we feel happy, every part of our lives seems a little bit better.

Second, you find yourself becoming a seeker. My observation about seeking is that most people find what they seek. It's uncanny. So you generally find what you become interested in. Once you start that process, you're likely to become a seeker on a more consistent basis. Now you don't wonder if something is real; you go out and find it. For instance, I was interested in words when I was young. I would ask my parents what a word meant, and they would tell me, "Go look it up." I became quite a student of vocabulary because I was constantly looking up words in the dictionary. That drove my interest in reading and writing, which I'm still very interested in today.

Interested people are all seekers. Seekers follow their curiosity and want to know everything about their particular interest. They stay up late reading, participate in focused online communities, and spend hours searching for information and/or practicing skills connected to their interest.

Some people decide to become seekers, and others just have that inclination naturally the minute they come into the world. People who love to read books all seem to have this seeking trait built into them. They love to read and learn. It's like a balm for their minds and souls.

Seeking is a desire, at the end of the day. I believe this is a gift that we can give to ourselves. Not only is it a wonderful way to make sure you spend some time in this important Slice of your life, but it has wonderful benefits. Every person I have known who is a seeker seems to stay young and youthful no matter the person's age.

Positive energy and a seeking mindset contribute to a better sense of perspective. Moreover, when your energy level isn't depleted and you feel as though you're always making progress in something, the stress of everyday life is less likely to feel overwhelming. Your life seems calmer and more manageable.

WHAT KIND OF THINKER ARE YOU?

Now, how do we access our Intellectual Slice so we can receive the benefit? First, look at your own thinking tendencies and preferences. Since we all communicate every day with the people in our lives, we are all thinking, all the time. Our brains are "on" 24 hours a day, even when we are sleeping. Like the heart, the brain is always working on our behalf.

Herrmann International, a privately held management consulting company, has done a great deal of research about the thinking process and has conducted millions of surveys around the world. I'm a licensed practitioner from Herrmann International, and one of its tools that I use in my work is the HBDI profile.

According to the HBDI profile tool, our thoughts fall into one or more of four categories: what, how, who, and why.[3] Each category is characteristic of a major thinking style.

Interestingly, most of us have distinct thinking preferences. Learning your thinking preference is extremely helpful when you want to rekindle or inspire your curiosity. The following descriptions will help you determine what kind of thinker you are:

- **What.** People who prefer to think in the "what" category like facts, information, analysis, and data. If you are a "what" person, you like the details about the world that is all around you. When answering questions, you review the available information first and then determine what is most logical. Without this process, you are not satisfied and are often frustrated with the lack of attention others pay to the simple questions in life. The hallmark of this thinking style is critical thinking, often the preference of attorneys, engineers, and scientists.

- **How.** Those who prefer to think about the "how" first are similar to the other three types but also a little different. These folks are drawn to a process first. If you are a "how" person, you like to put things in order with a plan that has a beginning, middle, and end. You find yourself most comfortable when your daily to-do list has sequential order—up to and including spontaneity! Since you are so organized, you are often found in businesses that require the management of offices, functions, and execution.

- **Who.** The "who" thinkers are quite different from their what and how neighbors. Their preference is to think about people and interpersonal feelings first. If this is your preference, you are comfortable with and recognize how other people are feeling every day. You find it easy to "read" the room and empathize very quickly with a person who is confused or struggling. People matter, and the reasons are always noticeably clear for you to see. Therefore, you're the person who's able to apply and attach feelings to facts and process. In addition, your intuition is usually very strong. You are most comfortable in an organization where you can lead and manage people. You enjoy being of service and need people to reenergize yourself.

- **Why.** "Why" people always think about the big picture first. If you are a "why" person, you want to know the purpose behind what people are doing and why they are doing it. Your comfort level is with the future and wondering what direction this task or subject in the present moment will lead. In addition, your tendency is to think about how everything connects. You are comfortable with ideas, concepts, and risk taking. Most importantly, you need any job or work you do to be fun!

There is interesting data surrounding these thinking styles. Of the millions of people surveyed to determine their thinking preferences, only 3 percent of people prefer to think in all four of the thinking styles. Only 5 percent of people prefer to think in just one style. However, 34 percent of people prefer to think in three of those styles, and the largest group of people, 58 percent, prefer to think in two of those primary styles.[4]

Understanding your thinking preferences is important because your preferences dictate your curiosity. Everyone has at least some intrinsic curiosity, of course, but what someone pursues is typically tied to his or her thinking preferences.

Understanding your interests helps you to be comfortable being curious because the desire to learn will come more naturally.

In each thinking category, there are dozens of things to be interested in and worth pursuing. The what-style thinkers like to learn how things work and the logical steps to follow in order to learn. That applies to literally any skill, from learning how to make frosting to learning how to play the trumpet. I have seen people who prefer this thinking style decide to learn how to build a tree house for their children. They've never built anything before in their lives, but in their way of thinking, there are facts, materials, and a logical instruction process. If they've got a blueprint or tutorial to follow, they're off with hammer in hand.

The how-style thinker is also teeming with possibilities. Learning how things work and enjoying the process of learning gives you consistent and fulfilling feelings of satisfaction, success, and enjoyment. Again, the how thinking preference can be applied to a number of areas, from improving a volunteer nonprofit in your local community to learning how to coach your daughter's youth soccer team.

The who-style thinker would more than likely lead your curiosity toward an endeavor or idea that has something to do with people. Since there are so many people who need us, your opportunities are boundless. I have observed that many who thinkers enjoy volunteering to help other people. Who thinking combines the need to be around other people with the need to do something that feels good.

The why people among us tend to want to learn big subjects and ideas. Often, they are creative. Their intellectual curiosity leads them to explore things that have great meaning to them. This can often manifest in ventures like starting up a community theater all the way to organizing a townwide campaign to support a good cause.

The end goal is big, exciting, and fun for why people. They tend to love what they do, so it doesn't feel like "work" to them.

In short, the Intellectual Slice can expand your thinking, interests, and knowledge of the world and the people in it. Make sure not to let it slip away.

SLICE CASE STUDY: DAN

Dan was a character, one of a kind in many ways.

A year and a half after Dan's company sold a controlling share to a private equity (PE) firm, I was contacted by the firm to help Dan with his leadership and communication skills. His manufacturing company, which had been doing quite well, had stalled shortly after the transaction. While that is not unusual, the performance of the company continued to decline, and something had to be done.

Dan had stayed on as president and CEO after he had sold the controlling share to the PE firm. He had been working with a new senior executive team for the past year and a half. The PE firm referred to Dan's communication style as "occurring only on a need-to-know basis," which was at first was mildly amusing, but was now a problem.

A large man, Dan was an introvert who, just as the PE firm alleged, rarely spoke unless he thought you needed to know something about what he was doing or thinking. He had never spent time with someone like me, who works with executives on talent development. He was a self-starter and a self-made businessperson. He was born and raised in the Midwest, studied engineering at a Midwestern college, and got a job in product development right out of school. Early in his career, he realized he had a knack for finding innovative solutions to customer problems. He cofounded the company with a partner who was extremely gregarious and a natural leader of people—which at first complemented Dan's style nicely (and perhaps compensated for his shortcomings). Fifteen years later, however, they went separate ways, with Dan buying his partner out. Shortly after, Dan sold the controlling interest to the PE firm.

Dan was simply brilliant. His brain worked constantly, and he could solve customer problems and figure things out no matter how complex. He never stopped until the problem was solved. That is, he was brilliant in everything except for people.

You've probably met a "Dan." It was clear after our first few meetings that Dan could not figure out people and their motivations. For example, Dan's direct reports would want to make what they thought was a pretty simple decision: for instance, whether or not to invest money in a new plant machine. The team had already done its research, and everyone agreed the new plant machine was necessary (as the old broken one was already causing time delays). Dan's process was the antithesis of the team's process.

Dan had to grind through every single detail before he could decide. That frustrated the team, who just needed him to make the decision. Dan would insist, "I know I'm right—there's a lot to think about. You're being too quick and fast with the facts." This happened all the time.

In working with the new executive team, Dan's inability to read the room created tension. When speaking, Dan simply did not have the ability to see when his message was not being received. Dan would walk out of a meeting saying, "That was a very good meeting because I gave them all of the right information that they needed to have."

When I'd follow up with the executive team members, however, I would discover he missed the mark entirely. They had been distracted and confused by what he was saying and couldn't follow him at all. That's a problem in a leadership role—you need to know when people are with you and when they become disengaged.

The people who had been with him in the company from the beginning loved him. They spoke highly of him and referred to his awkwardness with people as well meaning and "just Dan being Dan." To them he was that lovable uncle you wanted to see at Christmas but who said four words the whole day.

But now, of course, Dan's circle had widened. The new people who had come to the company had no idea what to make of Dan and his leadership and communication style.

As a result, the tension level on Dan's executive team was growing, and the members on the team were making rumblings to the PE firm about the need to take action to improve the situation. As you might guess, this made for a three-ring circus of stress between Dan, the executive team, and the PE firm. Dan was extremely frazzled, and he needed some help.

Since the pressure was on to resolve the business and leadership issues, I decided that incorporating the Seven-Slice Method might be the most practical solution. Dan was very process-oriented—a how-style thinker according to the HBDI profile we shared earlier in the chapter. He liked things in a sequential order that he could understand and appreciate. I had a feeling he would latch onto the Seven-Slice approach and figure out how he could use it best. I explained the method to Dan and suggested that the urgency here was the fact that he had to improve his communication skills before the leadership skills would make any difference with his team. And to do that, he had to be calm enough to learn new things (and at this time in his life, he was anything but calm).

Dan took to this in a very matter-of-fact way. He discussed some personal things that were going on in the Slices of his life without emotion or embarrassment, and he was determined to see if the Seven-Slice Method could help get him to a better place in his business and personal life. Here is what his profile looked like:

- **The Family Slice.** His four adult children were all in very different stages of their lives. Each had struggles and ups and downs, but they had a good relationship with their father.

  Dan's marriage was another story. He and his wife had been married for almost 25 years, and though his wife thought the marriage was going just "fine," Dan had been unhappy for years. His wife shut down any conversation about their marriage beyond discussions around their children and various home improvement projects (which apparently were constantly being done on their property).

  That seemed serious. When I asked Dan if he had ever had a real conversation with his wife about his unhappiness, his answer was a declarative no.

  His wife was a chatty, happy person. Her glass wasn't just half full, but overflowing. Dan claimed he did not stand a chance in a conversation battle with her. He would stammer and stutter something, and his wife would shut it down. I asked how close he was to the end of his patience, and he indicated he had passed that point some time ago. This Slice took almost all the time in his life except what he put into his Professional Slice. He quantified it at 20 percent.

- **The Professional Slice.** Clearly the people issues were coming to a full boil right now, and Dan was struggling to learn how to manage it. This Slice was taking 75 percent of his time each week, including weekends.

- **The Personal Slice.** As he said, the business was his personal life at this stage of his life, but he knew that could not continue. He spent 5 percent of his time in this slice.

- **The Physical Slice.** Dan had not engaged in real physical activity to speak of for a long while. Years ago, he had a heart attack that required surgery. For a time afterward, he committed to losing weight to maintain a healthier lifestyle and manage issues like blood pressure and so forth. However, he'd fallen back to his old habits. He now devoted no time to his Physical Slice.

- **The Intellectual Slice.** Dan said intellectual pursuits had been and continued to be a constant part of his life. He read almost every day. While he enjoyed learning very much, none of his reading fed his Personal Slice. He was more concerned with staying on top of current market trends and the financial markets. Furthermore, if someone on his team asked a question that he didn't know the answer to, he would thoroughly research the subject to learn about it and respond very quickly. He could not put a percentage of time he devoted to this Slice since it was so ingrained in his whole life.

- **The Emotional Slice.** This Slice "had a vacancy sign on it," to use Dan's phrase. He claimed he never thought about his emotional life. I pointed out he m might ay be thinking about it more often than he thought when he examined his marriage and his "feelings" there. He said he spent zero percent in this Slice.

- **The Spiritual Slice.** Dan considered himself spiritual but not religious. He was raised a Protestant and attended church services with his wife and children for many years. Today, he only attended services for holidays or weddings. I asked if he read in this Slice of his life. He used to, but that too had drifted as the stress in the business kept rising.

Dan's Plan

Given Dan's strengths and where he was most apt to devote time in order to address the two areas that were causing him the most stress, we decided that a crash course in how to manage people and develop emotional intelligence would benefit him the most. That meant I would spend a good deal of one-on-one time with him in the coming weeks and would be providing him a copious number of articles and books to devour on this subject. Given that this was all going into his Intellectual Slice, Dan was energized and optimistic that this might be a way through this challenging spot in his life.

As you can see, Dan's experience was different from that of many of the other people you've met in this book. In the short term, we used a targeted approach. But as is often the case, when you focus attention on the area of your life that needs the most work, other things emerge. In Dan's case, through the process of learning more about why people do what they do and improving his own emotional intelligence, he learned a great deal about himself and his own emotions. Ultimately, that newly acquired self-knowledge helped Dan resolve about half the issues he was wrestling with.

Within two to three months, Dan had opened up and was asking questions that previously would have been way outside his comfort zone. He had started to become more aware of the feelings and emotions in other people, and he wanted to spend more time on these "people" subjects as they related to the business issues that were bubbling up.

Dan took a very literal approach to his self-development in this area and chose to think his way through it. He explained he was more likely to persist if he could make a list of tasks that would help him start connecting better with the people in the company that reported to him and with the PE firm people.

What worked here for Dan was simple, and the same approach probably would work for anyone who prefers to think and act in a literal style. On the other hand, this would not work as well for a person who prefers a more conceptual thinking style. Dan knew himself well enough to declare that the literal approach would be the right one for him.

Using the tools that are available in emotional intelligence training, we profiled each person on his executive team so that Dan could start to "read" them better during their meetings. Prior to this, the feedback regarding Dan was that he could appear to be "tone deaf" or disengaged at times. He needed to turn that around by addressing what each person was thinking before he would chime in with his opinion or prescribe a solution to a problem that people should be responsible for.

The second part was to focus on the process of how the meetings were conducted. This was due to feedback about Dan that suggested he could be strong-willed and stubborn about the agenda in team meetings. To create more connection and followership for Dan with others on his team, he had to change this pattern and become more open about receiving input and addressing the interests of team members.

This literal approach worked for Dan. He deliberately sought out input from each team member before the weekly team meetings. The input from the team moved the agenda to broader subjects and away from the technical issues that Dan always emphasized.

This step alone reduced the tension level right away. People want to feel heard, and when they saw Dan taking concrete steps to address and integrate their feedback, their attitude toward him improved. Over the next six months or so, the team dynamic continued to move in the right direction, and Dan learned more about the differences between the members of his team. In the past, he had treated everyone the same, as if one size fits all.

This new, well-received approach made a positive difference in his Professional Slice. But now something started to happen in another area of his life. Suddenly, Dan was on a new mission.

Due to this experience of learning more about people and what they were thinking and feeling, Dan's own Emotional Slice began to awaken. This reminds me of the expression, *Be careful what you wish for!* The experience of learning more about his feelings set him on a course for learning how to navigate the conflicts he had with people. Previously, whenever a conflict surfaced, Dan would either avoid it and hope it went away or stubbornly use a passive-aggressive approach to "win" the conflict situation. Neither strategy worked particularly well for him, and now he saw a chance to address his interpersonal conflicts with an expanded toolbox.

Dan began to practice dealing with small conflicts by using the emotional intelligence approach. First, he examined his self-awareness of a conflict and then asked the other party what that person's awareness level was in order to determine if there was a real conflict or simply poor communication. For example, he and the marketing vice president would often disagree about various elements of a marketing campaign for some of the company's products. In the past, Dan would say, "No, we're not going to do it that way.

We're going to do it this way, and I want you to do it now." He would say it in a flat, unemotional way, but it would trigger anger and frustration in the vice president, who believed Dan wasn't listening to him.

This is emotional intelligence (or a lack of it) at work—Dan didn't recognize the marketing vice president was frustrated.

As Dan increased his emotional intelligence, he started approaching these situations by saying something like, "I see it this way—tell me why you think the plan you have is effective and will be successful."

In essence, he started by hitting the pause button and allowed the other person to articulate his or her point of view. Dan would listen, which is what the other party wanted more than anything else. Then Dan was able to say: "I hear you, and I like parts of it. What do you think of these suggestions that would change it a bit?"

What had been conflict became a negotiation. Dan would walk away from such meetings less frustrated, and so would the marketing executive. We call that a win-win.

As he practiced, a truth hit Dan like a ton of bricks: he had a habit of not being honest with himself or others. For years, he had avoided his Emotional Slice in order to not disappoint people or cause more rancor and discord in his home and business environments.

Even when he felt hurt or disagreed with a course of action, he would say he was fine. By being dishonest and soldiering on, Dan was inadvertently sabotaging any chance of getting his needs met and denying the other party a true opportunity to work with him.

His studies taught him that while few people are comfortable dealing with conflict, there are benefits to being honest in our relationships. The air gets cleared, and often the problem leading to the conflict has a reasonable solution that can make moving forward easier and potentially more enjoyable.

As for the Spiritual Slice, Dan decided the best way to proceed was to revisit it with his grandchildren, two of whom were about the age where going to a church service would be an appropriate activity for them to do together. Though he needed a few weeks to prioritize his work issues, he eventually incorporated going to church with his grandchildren regularly, to everyone's enjoyment and enrichment.

The conclusion to Dan's journey took another year to fully play itself out. First, after a year, Dan concluded that the business needed someone other than himself to run it. Though he improved his people skills and developed a more positive leadership style, he found himself just having lost the "fire" for the business that had previously driven him to want to work hard to build a successful company. Though the conversation with the PE firm wasn't easy, and executing the separation was complicated, eventually a new CEO was recruited, and Dan stayed on as a member of the board of directors. Rather than feeling sad or missing the role he once played, all he felt was relief—which indicated he'd made the right choice for himself and his business.

Next, he addressed his Family Slice. He spoke directly with his spouse about where he thought the marriage was and what his feelings were about the marriage going forward. At first, his wife declared that Dan had clearly lost his mind. Her position was that they had a wonderful life, and if he was no longer in love with her, then his feelings were simply wrong. In the past, Dan would have accepted someone else's diagnosis of his own feelings and soldiered on in misery. But now that he had learned to own his emotions, he knew he owed it to both of them to respect his wife's perspective, but not to pretend he didn't have his own. Eventually, they dissolved the marriage. Today, Dan is happy, remarried, consulting part-time for companies around the United States, and sailing his boat.

On the surface, Dan went far by focusing on only two or three Slices in his life. However, the dire place he was in when he and I first started working together demonstrates that two or three Slices just wasn't enough. Dan used this method in his own way to find himself and learned how to make decisions that reduced the stress and chaos in his life. Later, opening the possibility of letting his other Slices enter his life more often allowed him to find his version of happiness.

CHAPTER SUMMARY

When your curiosity level increases, your attitude is likely to improve as well. With an engaged mind and positive attitude, it's easier to find motivation to make positive changes in your life.

The thing to remember about the value proposition in the Intellectual Slice is that it's a starting point for your own curiosity—but there's potentially no ending point. The meaning here is that you can continue a lifetime journey of learning things once you catch the spark. As we've talked about, curiosity often becomes a low priority for people because the busyness of life seems to replace it.

It may be helpful to use this Slice as a reminder. Once a week, ask yourself, "Have I learned something new?" It's a cliché, but in my own life I try to learn one thing new per day from one of my clients. Since I talk with so many people each day, I made it a goal. In this small way I've trained my brain to look for new things every day. Like anything else, it's a habit now. So perhaps in your own small way you can find something once a week or once a month that's new. Just remind yourself to start looking for it—it might work.

THE EMOTIONAL SLICE

First note to self in this Slice: *Emotions. We all have them.* Addressing your Emotional Slice is about noticing your emotions and understanding how to manage them for your own benefit.

Due to time pressures and life challenges, many people find themselves spending little time in the Emotional Slice. However, this is an area of our lives that can truly benefit us if we pay attention to it, and conversely, it can lead us to great harm if we ignore it too long.

Our emotional life is an enormous subject—so for our purposes, we will limit our discussion to identifying our emotions, thinking about them, and showing how your emotions can become a source of refuge from the stress that is bottled up in the other Slices, particularly in the Family and Professional Slices. In addition, we will discuss how to develop your emotional intelligence to help you achieve harmony with your other Six Slices of your life.

WE ALL HAVE EMOTIONS

Since we all share many of the same emotions, it is a good idea to identify them. This is important, because we want to spend enough time in the Emotional Slice so that we can understand our emotions and learn to manage them in every area of our lives.

We all share the emotions of joy, sadness, anger, surprise, disgust, contempt, fear, and excitement.

Each of these emotions has nuance depending on the circumstances that brought the emotion about. For instance, a loved one dying and a canceled vacation might both bring about some sadness, but the depth, duration, and impact on your life will be different.

There is also irony in this Slice of our lives. Our emotions are our own in that you don't share them with anyone. In other words, when you're angry, the person next to you doesn't share the exact same angry experience. Yet our emotions directly impact the people all around us, especially our friends and family. In fact, those around us are often more aware of our emotions than we are.

I am sure we have all known someone with anger issues. And when that person is given direct or indirect feedback that the anger is a problem, he or she often brushes it off with something like, "Oh I know I have a temper, but that's just me ... !" In essence, the message is, *You deal with it so I don't have to!* Which, of course, exacerbates situations where this person's anger is impacting someone else.

Alternatively, a parent might come home from work angry about something that happened earlier in the day. The parent's anger affects everyone else in the house. The other people in the family feel it. The negative emotion pushes family members away. Conversely, the parent who comes home thrilled because something went well at work also affects everyone in the house.

Many methods are available to help you navigate the process of learning and understanding emotions and how to manage them. You can consult with a mental health professional. You can speak with friends, clergy members, or people in support groups to get a different perspective on your emotions and how they are perceived by others. You can also read about emotions and work on managing your thoughts to better understand the role emotions play in your life. The purpose is to elevate your level of understanding.

As mentioned above, many people avoid their Emotional Slice. While there are many possible reasons, the two reasons I've seen in my practice that are the most common are, one, lack of time and, two, success in other facets of life. These two reasons seem to resonate with the people I work with and particularly, men. Generally, women seem more open to the value of appreciating their emotional lives. At the same time, many people struggle when time and success interfere with the process of carving out the time and interest for the emotional well-being they want.

BARRIERS TO ENGAGING WITH
THE EMOTIONAL SLICE

We can all appreciate the time component issue. Getting in touch with and learning how to better navigate and manage our emotions requires a time commitment. And we often feel too busy. When our lives are full of commitments and responsibilities, there is a cadence that simply promotes that rhythm to continue. We might like the idea of changing our busy, pressure-filled, overscheduled lives, but over time we get used to it. Moreover, many people rationalize, who has the time to read a book about emotions? Who has the time to seek and work with a mental health professional or counselor?

Another interesting characteristic I've noticed in my clients is that even when they *want* the busyness of their lives to slow down, they hesitate to do anything about it, including prepare themselves emotionally to for the hoped-for life change. After observing this over many years, I've identified success as often being the root cause for that hesitation.

The success, I've noticed, can come in many forms. Career advancement is the most prevalent. The path upward in an organization is rarely simple and never easy. It requires years of dedication and an emotionally draining commitment level—all of which leaves less motivation to invest energy and interest anywhere else, but particularly in their emotional lives.

Financial growth is also an occasional obstacle to fully engaging with the Emotional Slice. It cuts both ways in some cases. When someone's income is increasing, it can be tempting for them to conflate financial growth with harmony. In other words, they rationalize that *if I am financially successful and flourishing, I must be doing fine in every area of my life ... right?* And under that logic, why would financially successful people need to address their emotional life?

On the other side, people who struggle financially might feel restricted, as though their world is shrinking, because their thoughts are consumed by a lack of prosperity.

THE EMOTIONAL IMPORTANCE OF RECOGNITION

One source of emotion that gets little attention is recognition. The recognition is both spoken and upspoken. No one wants to feel invisible. No one wants to be taken advantage of. It's a complaint that many people have their entire lives—in work, friendships, family, and volunteer activities. For their entire lives, people want to be recognized on some level.

And by that I don't mean people want or need a parade in their honor—they just want a gesture of recognition. A thank you. An affirmation that their work is appreciated.

When that's not given, people respond in specific ways. Some people become resentful; some people become rude; others become dismissive. In my work, I try to remind my clients that the people around them want to be recognized for what they do.

In fact, a study from Boston Consulting Group (which surveyed over 200,000 people) revealed that the number one factor in employee happiness was being appreciated for their work. Salary was all the way down at number eight.[1]

Have you been recognized recently for something you did or helped with? Did you notice how it felt?

Are there people in your life that you could give a little more recognition to for their contributions? How do you think they would feel if you did?

When you are succeeding in your Professional Slice, it can be quite intoxicating. Our sense of well-being increases, our confidence soars, and we are often sought after for advice and more responsibility.

Meanwhile, the Emotional Slice is not on the radar screen of our lives. That has consequences. When your perspective is unbalanced, you're more likely to overreact or underreact in everyday situations. In other words, if I'm struggling and unhappy with something in my life but I don't acknowledge the source of how I'm feeling, I'm more likely to fly off the handle when someone commits a minor infraction. For instance, someone might cut me off in traffic, and I could react inappropriately because I lack perspective on the size and import of the actual event.

A great exercise when you find yourself getting upset is to ask, "How should I feel about this right now? Is it worth getting upset about?"

Maybe it is—but maybe it isn't. I have found that people who spend little to no time in the Emotional Slice struggle with perspective because they tend to only see their own.

One of my favorite questions to ask when businesspeople are upset with their team or an individual is, "Let me ask you this—how do you think *they're* feeling about it right now?"

It's a question that makes people step out of themselves and into another person's shoes. Some people respond, "I don't care about how they're feeling; this is how *I* feel."

You really don't have the luxury to take that stance. You might not like what others feel; how about that? Now we're in a real pickle. At this point, it's hard to find that pause button to put yourself in the right place emotionally so that you don't sound problematic.

People who don't spend a lot of time in their Emotional Slice in business are often the same people that we are afraid to bring bad news to. They tend to overreact and kill the messenger, so to speak. That's not just uncomfortable—it can have real consequences. If everyone knows the boss has an anger problem, the team might hide or conceal information that wreaks havoc down the road.

All that to say: success does not automatically mean that you have a healthy emotional life. Without some introspection and understanding of our emotions, we can go to an extreme part of our self and lose a bigger and more important part of who we are as the result of unbridled success.

Another powerful emotional barrier that can often develop with successful people: their ability to listen to constructive feedback diminishes—particularly when it comes from people who they think do not know how difficult it is to achieve. For example, a person with this barrier might respond defensively to constructive feedback from his or her spouse: "I'm being short with the kids? Let me tell you how hard I'm working . . . " Or if your boss tells you that you're being rude to your team, you might bristle: "Why don't you ask our clients if I need to work on rudeness. Do you like all the new clients I'm bringing in?" Even though your spouse is not talking about how hard you work, and even though your boss is not talking about how you handle your clients, you act as though they are.

In a way, there is a sense of logic in that illogic. *Since becoming successful in the Professional Slice requires everything in a person's life, the entirety of my life must also be in great shape!* Whenever I have seen this perspective surface in a dialogue, it is safe to assume that the person spends little time in the Emotional Slice. The Emotional Slice is where we learn to manage our emotions around success, failure, confidence, and self-esteem. It is also the place in our lives where our most important reality exists. If we're emotionally healthy, we don't get fooled by appearances and succumb to the temptation to lose sight of what matters most in our lives beyond professional and material success.

Emotion and Reason—at Odds?

A final observation about what keeps us from spending some time in this Slice of our life is the battle some profess that reason and emotion cannot exist simultaneously. This is the classic argument between left-brain and right-brain thinkers.[2] The left-brain folks subscribe to the notion that emotion is a hindrance to progress. This is because they believe that decision-making, judgment, and analysis cannot function if emotion is interjected into that process. On the other side of the argument are the right-brain thinkers who contend that only by understanding how people feel about the decisions, judgments, and analysis can you possibly be successful.[3]

It is a tug-of-war many organizations experience from time to time. In most practical applications, you need both to holistically deliver the right information, perspective, and impact that our decisions, judgments, and analysis are trying to achieve. But even people who believe they are driven by reason above all else still have emotions. They're just not attending to their Emotional Slice or acknowledging their emotions in any meaningful way. This is valuable for all of us to keep in mind, regarding both ourselves and the people in our lives.

BENEFITS OF LIVING MORE IN YOUR EMOTIONAL SLICE

Volumes of studies have been conducted to measure and assess the benefits of understanding emotions. These studies involve people of every age group, from young children to our senior citizens.[4, 5]

Having absorbed many of these studies and observed in my own practice the value of knowing more about the emotional life we live, there seem to be two main benefits that are universally recognized from in these studies: self-development and healthier relationships. Let's look at why that might be true as you spend time in this Emotional Slice.

Engaging with your Emotional Slice feeds your self-development because you're more likely to understand why you feel what you feel and to be consistent in your attitude and behavior. Just take two of the more common emotions we all share, happiness and sadness. Most people react about the same when it comes to the big events that affect all of us. We all are happy when our home team wins the championship, and we all are sad when the home team loses the championship. Of course, that only happens one way or the other once a year.

But in our day-to-day lives, these two emotions can regularly occur, particularly if there's a great deal of conflict. For example, if things are going wonderfully at home with your children, marriage, and lifestyle, but your job life is clearly going sideways—well, there is potential for dichotomous feelings (and therefore behavior). This daily whipsaw of emotions is not healthy and not sustainable over a long period of time.

The solution to this challenge is to attain a good emotional perspective in the moment. Easy for me to say, I know. In reality, how can you find perspective, or preferably already have perspective, in order to address the conflict in your life? The answer is to spend enough time in your Emotional Slice to understand what's important to you and how those things can produce feelings of happiness and sadness.

The first thing you learn when you get acquainted with your emotions is that all your feelings are OK, meaning whatever you are feeling is legitimate. The work that one must do in this process is to then figure out if your feelings are appropriate to the situation, circumstance, or person causing you to feel what you're feeling.

The benefit is not making bad feelings go away; rather, the benefit is learning how to manage your feelings in the moment better by understanding why you are feeling what you are feeling. It helps to take the emotional roller coaster ride out of the equation.

We are not looking for perfection in this Slice. We are looking for a better way to handle the regular occurrences of stress and conflict in our lives. This won't happen overnight, but over time (and with effort), all of us can learn to manage life better by managing our feelings better as we grow and evolve.

The second benefit of managing emotions better is healthier relationships—a goal that is on many people's wish lists. This benefit is comforting on several levels. "Healthier" is not necessarily looking for perfect. That is a distinction worth remembering. I suppose there are perfect relationships out there, but they are few, for certain.

I work a great deal with people in business relationships, particularly around the subject of conflict. All of us manage to get into some interpersonal conflict from time to time. When that happens, there is a real desire to tell the other person to *just change!* Just do the dishes instead of leaving them in the sink or all over the house; just be on time for every meeting from now on; just get your paperwork in on time; just stop dismissing every new idea out of hand.

That rarely works, which has led to the cliché we have all heard: *People don't change.* That's not terribly optimistic for those of us who wish we could handle conflict better or who must work and/or live alongside people who don't handle conflict well. However, there is another behavioral axiom about people changing their behavior. It goes something like this: *If you want to change the other person's behavior . . . change your behavior first.*

The first step in changing your behavior is changing how you think about a subject or situation that you are set in your ways about. For example, say your spouse wants you to do the grocery shopping once a month, and you typically complain because it's terribly inconvenient given your business schedule. But instead of telling your spouse about your feelings or refusing to do it, you decide to say: "I'll do it the first Monday every month," and you put it in your schedule as though it's a business meeting. Once it's on your official schedule, you start seeing the activity as a necessary contribution to your household rather than a form of punishment.

This likely has a ripple effect. You feel better because you no longer have anything to complain about; you just do it. The hope is that you receive recognition and appreciation back at the house and your spouse's behavior toward you changes in a positive way.

What comes first, thoughts or feelings? I'm not sure in every instance, but in general I believe it's easier to change how we think about a subject or person if we start with how we *feel* about the subject or person first. To do that, we need to have access to our feelings. To have access, we need to spend time in our Emotional Slice. We need to take stock of our feelings and think about how we feel and why we feel the way we do. With that level of understanding, we can then decide to change what we feel and think about that emotion.

This is common in conflict resolution where two people decide that what made them very frustrated and angry is now a negotiation. How can that happen? By the two people learning to slow down, examine their feelings, and understand the consequences of their feelings. From there, they can think about what feelings would have to change to produce a better outcome.

This process is also part of the building blocks of your level of Emotional Intelligence.

EMOTIONAL INTELLIGENCE

Our level of emotional intelligence (or EQ—emotional quotient) is widely viewed as a very accurate measurement for your success in working with people across any organization, group, or family.[6] It is used in many businesses and in family therapy practices. Though a big subject for our purposes here, I would like to provide a short explanation of the basic tenets of EQ so we can use it when we spend time in our Emotional Slice.

Emotional intelligence consists of competencies across four different areas: self-awareness, self-management, social awareness, and relationship management. In each area you can assess your level on a 0-to-10 scale, with 0 meaning that you have no competencies in the area and 10 meaning that you have a strong command of the area. This allows you to look at your EQ as a quotient that can help explain why some relationships work well and others do not.

Working with these competencies not only helps improve your EQ; it provides a kind of road map for exploring your Emotional Slice, particularly if that's an overlooked part of your life. Each of the four competencies is described below.

Self-Awareness

Having a healthy amount of self-awareness means that you recognize your strengths and weaknesses (and how they come across to others) accurately. You've probably met people with an extremely low score in self-awareness. They're the type of people who, even though they have never once turned their work in on time, inexplicably brag about how they pride themselves on their reliability and punctuality. When you have a high level of self-awareness, you can objectively evaluate yourself, manage your emotions well, and understand accurately how others perceive you.

Self-Management

Self-management is generally regarded as the ability to self-regulate, meaning how you modulate your thoughts, emotions, and actions in an environment involving people and responsibilities. Someone who scores high in self-management typically demonstrates self-confidence, patience, respect, maturity, and dependability. Someone low in self-management might interrupt others, overshare, and otherwise communicate inappropriately in a public setting and inadvertently embarrass others in conversation. Essentially low self-management often comes down to a demonstrated lack of maturity in certain business or social situations.

Social Awareness

Social awareness is your ability to perceive and empathize with people who are different from you. Also included in this regard is the ability to accurately "read" a room and how people are reacting. Some people are just naturally intuitive; others learn social awareness through experience and interacting with others over time. People who are socially aware can detect right away in a room full of people whom to approach and how to create a connection and rapport. They have an ability to adapt to the people they're engaging with. People without social awareness tend to act the same way with everyone, so as a result they do not connect as often with people who are different than they are. For example, people with low social awareness might avoid going to a cocktail party where there will be people they don't know, because they don't socialize with strangers easily. People with high social awareness look forward to those same parties.

Relationship Management

Relationship management reflects your interpersonal interest levels. People with a low score in relationship management struggle with relationships that aren't transactional or that have a tactical angle (for example, you might be "friends" with your neighbors because they have a pool, not because you actually like them). Such transactional relationships, as you can imagine, crumble at the first brush with conflict. People with a high score in this area have a genuine interest in the people who live and work around them, and they express a caring attitude. This enables them to continue to work well with others even when there is tension and conflict.

HOW YOU CAN USE EMOTIONAL INTELLIGENCE

Ideally you should score yourself and then ask someone you trust to evaluate you in each area as well (after all, if you lack self-awareness, how would you know?). If your scores (or the ones that have been given to you) aren't what you would like, then I encourage you to seek out other resources. And if your scores *are* where you'd like them to be, then I encourage you to learn more so that you can leverage such skills more effectively in everyday situations.

The reason I think nurturing and developing EQ is a useful tactic when exploring your Emotional Slice is because possessing competency in each of the four areas is transferable to your Family and Professional Slices. The time spent understanding your strengths and challenges in this emotional subject will serve you well whenever you are dealing with people and their emotions, as well as your own.

SLICE CASE STUDY: RANDALL

This next story is a little different in that the individual had a problem that required a medical professional to help solve. The Seven-Slice Method doesn't run counter to medical interventions—many of my clients have reported that the Seven-Slice Method proved to be an effective complement to other types of treatment. However, the Seven-Slice Method cannot (nor should it) *replace* clinical interventions.

Randall was a successful principal in his late forties in an engineering partnership firm. He was thoughtful, articulate, and a great negotiator. Smart, and often described as having a charming personality, Randall had a demeanor and communication style that earned him respect from both inside and outside the organization.

I'd worked with the managing partners at the firm for several years and had built a solid relationship with them. One day, I was asked to speak on a very confidential basis to one of the partners in the firm who was going through a difficult time in his life.

Randall had been struggling with depression for years but had never sought outside help for it. Recently, however, the symptoms had become a problem for him, and though his work in the firm was going fine, things at home with his wife and two young children were not.

At home he became very melancholy, meaning he wasn't dark, he wasn't angry—he was just consistently sad. It manifested in low energy and a lack of interest in things he used to be interested in, such as taking the kids down to the park on Sunday afternoons or going out to dinner with his wife. It was as though he'd lost interest in his life at home. There was no fighting or bickering; he was just sad and difficult to reach. His wife became quite concerned: *There's something wrong here, and I can't help you.*

He got the work done in terms of executing well and being productive and meeting deadlines, but again his lack of energy and his lack of interest in others were noticeable. His colleagues said he just appeared to be "different": "There's something wrong, but we just can't put our finger on it."

We've all seen that from time to time in others. It's the kind of behavior that has people asking: "Everything OK? You seem different lately."

Thinking he might need to take a leave of absence from the firm, Randall had approached the managing partners and shared his situation and concerns about moving forward. The partners' suggestion was to do whatever Randall's medical professionals recommended, but the company would love to see him continue to work as much or as little as he could while undergoing treatment. They hadn't—and wouldn't—share his situation with the rest of the firm. However, they suggested that he speak with me to get an additional perspective since I was experienced at helping people navigate acute life situations such as his.

Randall reached out to me and suggested that we sit down and discuss how we might work together in this moment. He outlined his history with depression, explaining that it had started in high school and continued through college—but after he finished graduate school, his symptoms seemed to recede. His wife was aware of his depression but had never witnessed the symptoms except for the occasional "blue Monday" kind of moment from time to time, and there was certainly no cause for alarm at that point.

About nine months before we met, the old symptoms had crept back, and they eventually increased in intensity until he knew he could no longer go it alone. Through his personal physician, he started regular sessions with a psychiatrist, but it was early days, and it would likely take weeks, months, even a year before he started seeing real progress.

I explained that I probably could not offer a lot except perhaps a new way to look at how he was going to move forward. I also reminded him that I couldn't step outside my scope of practice. I'm not a mental health professional and could not take the place of one. He understood. I suggested we explore the Seven-Slice Method.

A point worth making here is that most people find learning things about themselves to be both revealing and interesting. Some people have often pointed out that this process of thinking about the Seven Slices of their lives and answering the questions is a fun exercise. That can count for a lot when people are depressed or suffering from clinical depression and the world just seems a lot darker. The prospect of trying something new and having a little fun got Randall to smile for the first time since he could remember. He could point to every Slice and say, "I do this" or "I do that."

I was skeptical and followed up by asking him to shift the lens a bit. "What are you getting out of each Slice?" I asked.

Going Through the Motions

That got his attention. He realized he needed to understand what was going on in each Slice much more thoroughly. Once he considered each Slice again, he realized that yes, he was *technically* living in all the Slices. However, in most of the Slices, he was just going through the motions rather than participating with intent. That meant that he wasn't getting much out of them.

Right away he identified three Slices where he was going through the motions and receiving little to no reward: the Physical, Intellectual, and Spiritual.

In the Physical Slice he recognized that though he worked out on a treadmill a few times a week, he dreaded it and often cut his sessions short. As a result, he wasn't meeting his weight goals, and he wasn't in the shape he wanted.

In the Intellectual Slice, he noted that over the past five or six years, he only read for his legal interest needs and received no real thrill from learning much of anything new in his Intellectual Slice.

On the spiritual side, he was consistent in taking his family to synagogue regularly; however, it was more of a social experience, and he didn't feel he was building his spiritual life on any level.

Randall spent time in his Personal Slice by regularly having dinner parties and participating in other activities with a close circle of friends.

Randall loved his Family Slice and felt fortunate to have such a wonderful wife and two incredible children. He maintained good relationships with his parents and siblings and vacationed with them once every summer. His Professional Slice was also fine in that he liked his practice, his partners, and the firm. He wasn't passionate about his work, but he was someone who didn't feel a need to be passionate about how he paid the bills.

Which left his Emotional Slice. As Randall admitted, this is where he was suffering the most right now. I pointed out that he was dealing with that part of his life professionally, but since he was not a lifelong participant in psychotherapy, it would be worthwhile to think about what was going on in this part of his life in order to get the most out of the therapy as possible. We came up with a plan that might add to his improvement.

I suggested that he needed to start spending time in all his life Slices and to prioritize activities that would energize him, not just give him something to do. Going through the motions was not helping him, so maybe it was time to put together a different plan—one that would be simple and not require a big investment of time.

A New Plan

Randall gave this some thought, and a couple weeks later, he came back with a plan to move forward with different activities in each Slice of his life.

- **The Family Slice.** He was going to spend each Friday afternoon at home with his two children and each Friday morning with his wife doing whatever it is they wanted to do, even if it was nothing more than being with each other.

- **The Professional Slice.** Based on what he would be doing with his family, Randall would take Fridays off to be at home. He would delegate more of his work to the associates and other partners and would backfill if necessary on Sunday afternoons if the workload required it.

- **The Personal Slice.** He would keep it the same with a monthly dinner with two other friends in the city.

- **The Physical Slice.** He wanted to change it up, so he decided to swim twice a week at the sports club in the town he lived in. This would take place on the weekends, and his family would join him there once per month.

- **The Intellectual Slice.** He changed this up by buying the *New York Times* top-ten bestsellers and would read one per month for the next year.

- **The Emotional Slice.** He'd continue his therapy sessions, but with a focus on talking about all the areas of his life that he was now changing up to boost his energy and activity.

- **The Spiritual Slice.** He decided to reach out to his rabbi to talk about his situation and get the rabbi's input about his faith and how it might serve him during this difficult time.

The role he wanted me to play was "the reminder." We would meet a couple of times per month to check in and see if his plan was still on track. The first couple of months were a bit of a hit-and-miss situation, as he initially had difficulty sticking to the schedule he had set for himself. But by month three, he was in the groove and was fitting the plan in his lifestyle.

When it came to the impact on his emotional life, at first there was not much of a change. However, he began looking forward to the activities he set in motion each week. The swimming started to get him into better shape, and his daughters started tagging along with him a couple of times per month, which was great for them all. His Fridays at home went well. He and his wife took a number of short day trips that reminded Randall what it was like when they were first dating. The reading took some time to get going but eventually kicked in, as well. Late in the evening, he made it a point to read his 20 pages.

To Randall's surprise, the connection he made with his rabbi turned out to be incredibly positive. They had several things in common, including an interest in art history. They met once per month, and Randall felt this connection helped him personally and emotionally.

About a year later, the cloud lifted for Randall due to all the time and effort he put into working his way through that period. His therapy continued beyond that point, but his spirits had lifted. He went back to working Fridays, although he continued to prioritize time with his wife and kids on the weekend.

Again, the bulk of Randall's progress was due to his work with his psychiatrist. Making the shift from "going through the motions" to living a full emotional life is a process best aided by a licensed mental health professional. However, Randall believed that the Seven-Slice Method augmented his progress and helped him find his way back. It's been years since that time in his life, and he remains a happy and successful principal living a well-rounded, harmonious life with all the parts of it active and positive.

CHAPTER SUMMARY

There are several resources available should you ever find yourself in need of support in your emotional life. You should not feel as though there's any stigma attached to seeking help. There are therapists, counselors, and organizations available to you as a resource.

Since we all have emotions, it's probably a good reminder to check in with them once in a while for your own benefit given how easy it is to overlook them, put them aside, and then wait for the day they either implode or explode. It's been my experience working with many people that when they have easier access to their emotional life, they seem to be easier to relate to and far more comfortable admitting vulnerabilities, which makes them all the more human to the rest of us.

THE SPIRITUAL SLICE

The Spiritual Slice is the universal part of every human being. We all seek the meaning of life and want a connection to something bigger than us. It is a natural and normal response when we think about ourselves and our purpose in life.

This Spiritual Slice is about the inner you. This Spiritual Slice is where you can achieve a broader perspective on yourself and build your inner resolve and beliefs. Well-founded beliefs can serve us well in our Family and Professional Slices and help to make us better performers, better people, and more at ease with ourselves and how we conduct our lives.

For most of us, our spiritual beginning started in our family unit. Perhaps you remember being introduced to a religion by your family, being sent to a faith-based school, listening to grandparents talk about their spiritual lives, or simply being taught how to pursue your inner consciousness through meditation. The point is, we almost all have some sort of spiritual history to share, and we almost all seek a connection to our soul, or our inner self.

THE SPIRITUAL SLICE IS FOR EVERYONE

For thousands of years, people have been seeking their spiritual beliefs. The simple fact that there are over 4,200 different religions today suggests that the quest for a spiritual life is almost universal.

An ever-increasing number of people declared in recent polling surveys that they consider themselves "spiritual but not religious."[1] In essence, they are not affiliated with a specific religious organization but believe they have a spiritual life that they pursue in other ways. Others identify as atheists or as humanists and other groups that place humans at the center.

Of course, your Spiritual Slice does not have to be tied to any belief system or faith. If you are connecting with something bigger than you—whether that's nature, your purpose, your idea of God, or something else, you are attending your Spiritual Slice.

What's the value of pursuing a spiritual life? Your Spiritual Slice is a judgment-free zone that has the potential of providing you with a faith, a belief system, and an inner calm that can help restore your confidence and energy and better manage the tumult that surfaces in your life from time to time.

On a purely practical level, I have found many more people can speak to their other six Slices than they can speak to their Spiritual Slice. I suppose it may go back to the social guidelines that in polite society we don't speak about politics, sex, or religion. I don't disagree with that suggestion, mind you, but in the pursuit of finding more harmony in life, the Spiritual Slice is key.

The Spiritual Slice is where you nurture and carry your belief and faith. The time spent in your spiritual pursuits can provide the steadiness you need as you go through the stressful challenges in your life. Whether your spiritual life is defined by prayer, meditation, or chanting, it is an inner place that is real and beneficial for you.

The Spiritual Slice captures your beliefs, philosophies, and faith in things unseen—but are very real to you. With so many different religions, so many philosophies, and so many different thought leaders in this space, you have a world of choices in deciding what approach to embrace. Therefore, it is your own journey. You can pursue it in your own way. You may decide to join a community organization, become part of a small group of similar believers, or seek answers on your own through reading or meditation.

Many people I have spoken with about the Spiritual Slice say they would like to spend more time there but feel they are just too busy. As a result, it always ends up being something they will get to "tomorrow." And, of course, for many, tomorrow never comes.

ACCESSING YOUR SPIRITUAL SLICE

Whenever public figures stumble into scandals, whether in business, politics, or otherwise, they often say things like they "lost their way" or they "fell prey" to doing the wrong thing. "It's not who I am," some say. Or "I'm disappointed in myself."

I would suggest that who they are stems in part from their Spiritual Slice and what, if anything in life, they believe is bigger than they are. What is their spiritual connection to the world that keeps faith intact? Maybe when people "lose their way," it's because they've lost connection with their Spiritual Slice. We all lose our way from time to time, but people with a well-developed Spiritual Slice are better equipped to get back on their chosen path of life because they have faith it will bring them fulfillment and peace.

Where do your morals and values come from? Granted they come from lots of different places, but they often are most deeply felt in your Spiritual Slice. Accessing your Spiritual Slice can help you check in with yourself and see if you're acting in accordance with your values.

So how do we get there?

It certainly appears that the one requirement on which we need to spend time in the Spiritual Slice is quiet. I am not suggesting that noise is a problem, but rather our brains are never quiet. We are bombarded with so much information via television, social media, emails, texts, and news feeds every day, all day, that it becomes difficult to turn that barrage off in our brains. To begin to enter a meaningful moment in your Spiritual Slice, you must quiet your brain down long enough to let the peace of the present moment begin to find you.

Churches were many people's spiritual homes for centuries (and continue to be for many people today) because it is easier to quiet your thoughts when you are with others focusing on the same thing.[2] A scheduled time to meet to pursue a spiritual life makes total sense when you think about the busyness of the modern world.

While it might be hard to access your Spiritual Slice without any experience, it is certainly doable. You might find a quiet place outside or rely on the many smartphone applications out there that offer guided meditation or visualization.

In any case, if this is your first time taking time in the Spiritual Slice, then your first step should be to set your intention to spend a dedicated amount of time in this place. Then do the following:

- First, even as you begin, keep your thoughts in this Slice positive. You may wonder if this is real and have all sorts of doubts—but don't start thinking negatively about the effort. Decide that this is a pleasant or happy break from the rest of your too-busy life.
- Second, slow down your breathing and appreciate that if you take a few moments to yourself, your entire world will not come to a crashing halt

(though it might feel that way sometimes). Accessing your Spiritual Slice can improve your sense of perspective. Deep breaths have a way of calming the brain so you can start to hear your own thoughts. It only takes a few minutes, under three, and you can start to feel the rumble of noise in your brain (what I call RPMs) start to slow down.

For those of you who have had a history with your Spiritual Slice that did not go well, you are not alone. Perhaps you had a bad experience in a church or with your family of origin. Maybe you just drifted away as you got older and now wonder if it's worth the effort. If any of this describes you, I would suggest that you consider reconnecting with this Slice—but on your terms and in a way that works for you.

Many people have suggested that we are spiritual beings living a physical life rather than the other way around.[3] If that is true, it stands to reason there are great benefits to living more in your Spiritual Slice every day. In the Spiritual Slice, there is no concept of performance, competition, or measurement. For many people, the Spiritual Slice is where they can go to find peace and happiness at any time of the day. Others might find a sense of purpose and direction. It is entirely up to you to decide what you want from your time spent in your Spiritual Slice.

Many people find that meditation produces a heightened sense of ease and calmness that they can't find anywhere else in their lives. Others have built a belief and faith that steadies, comforts, and strengthens them when life takes them down difficult paths. Still others have found that taking time to enjoy the beautiful sights and sounds in nature allows them to escape their stress, gives them a moment of peace, and provides them what they need to better handle the challenges in their other life Slices.

It is important at this point to provide a perspective. I realize this subject is very deep and involved and people all over the world choose many different and sometimes complex paths in the quest for a stronger spiritual connection. If you haven't developed this side of yourself, I'm simply suggesting that you invest the amount of time and effort you need to find harmony and a feeling of balance in your life.

There is an additional benefit from spending time in the spiritual life that seems to be lacking in today's challenging times. I have seen many situations where this benefit has produced great successes. Conversely, I have seen situations where it is missing in individuals and teams, and they produce disappointing results. This additional benefit is *faith*.

Faith has been defined as the belief that something unknown and unseen is real. Faith often begins in individuals after they embark on a spiritual journey and develop the benefit of knowledge, belief, and trust that they are on the right path.

To build your faith in anything, there is a process. The first step typically involves reading and listening to gain a knowledge of the area. Some people will quickly conclude that the ideas they've read or heard about are, in fact, real and valid. Others will come to that conclusion much more slowly. After that, you have to see it work, feel it for yourself, and understand it in order for your trust to build to the point when you can declare, "I have faith that this will work for me."

When you have faith, you know that things will work out, even when it might look like they won't. Faith is not based on the tangible facts of the world. Faith comes from a belief in another reality, and the repeated experience of accessing that reality in your Spiritual Slice builds and strengthens your faith.

As it relates to real life, I have found inspiration and motivation spring from this Slice. I've noticed in working with many different people that those who spend little time in the Spiritual Slice, or those who were raised without any attention to it at all, have a consistently shallow level of faith. It surfaces when people don't believe in something that we must do or something that is going to happen. I've stumbled into it when I've said to a group of people, "You've just got to believe that this is going to happen because you've been working so hard on this." And they look at me and say, "What do you mean? Either things work or they don't. These are facts; it's success or failure."

Leaders who have a strong level of faith tend to be good at motivating people to take action.[4] Conversely, I have worked and witnessed very smart, talented people who don't have a background in faith and try to lead with motivation; most of the time, it does not work. People don't seem to buy it. It doesn't resonate; those leaders end up sounding too intellectual rather than visceral or emotional. It sounds practiced or rehearsed—not right or genuine.

In my experience, people who struggle with motivating others have little knowledge or experience in the Spiritual Slice of life. Many times, in family, business, social, and athletic endeavors, the facts suggest that we are in serious trouble. What keeps people motivated and inspired is often the leader or the leadership team members professing their belief that the goal is still attainable and that they will persist until it is achieved. Many of us learn these lessons when we are young, and they stick with us our entire lives.

So why does one person have this faith and another simply relies on facts or a process alone to achieve a result? I would suggest that faith that is born out of the time spent in one's Spiritual Slice gives people a perspective about the larger things in life, and that helps them to connect and motivate other people.

The Spiritual Slice helps us to answer the many questions we all have as we make our way through life. Deciding to spend some time there may be that critical key to finding harmony and success in the other Slices of your life.

SLICE CASE STUDY: MICHAEL

Michael was a 38-year-old investment banker living and working in Charlotte, North Carolina, with his wife. They had moved back to Charlotte after having spent the last 10 years in Manhattan where Michael worked at another investment banking firm. Michael had met his wife while they were both students at New York University, and part of their common bond was that they both hailed from North Carolina.

His wife, Heather, majored in marketing and had no trouble landing a job at a boutique firm in Manhattan. Michael found work at an investment firm. The next 10 years went by in a flash. They both enjoyed their work, enjoyed living in the city, and had good friends there. But both felt something was missing in their lives. They had married when they were both 32 years old. The wedding took place in North Carolina and was filled with family and friends. The question they were continually asked was, "When are y'all coming back home?" The question was starting to resonate.

About two years after their wedding, Michael and Heather decided to move back to the Charlotte area for many reasons. Heather found a part-time marketing position, and Michael landed a position in a prestigious midsize investment bank in Charlotte and was brought in with the understanding that within a few years he would be made a partner in the firm. He performed well, worked hard, and made a solid transition into the firm,

The investment firm was a client of mine, and I had the chance to meet Michael when he first started, but we had little contact over the next two years. The firm was doing very well, and Michael was part of the team; however, two years in, he hadn't risen to the level the senior partners had been expecting. Occasionally, they would wonder with me if there was something they could do to boost Michael's performance.

To the partners, the problem seemed to be he lacked the "fire" that one needs to be successful in that business. They informed me that they had suggested to him that he reach out to me and have a conversation about his progress to see if there was something we could do together to get him on an upward track.

In our first discussion, Michael shared that he enjoyed the firm and the people very much, which led him to believe that he had made a good decision to move back to North Carolina to raise a family. He also shared that his wife, Heather, was pregnant with their first child, and they were excited and happy that they had so many family members on both sides to help show them the ropes. In addition, he shared that she had left her part-time position and would become a full-time mom in several months. I asked how he felt about all of this.

"Oh," he laughed, "I'm feeling the pressure."

He meant that in a jocular way, but I have learned that it is always smart to poke around to see what is lurking behind humor when talking about serious life decisions.

In our next few meetings, we primarily focused on the firm's leadership style and the business deals Michael was working on that he hoped to close in that calendar year. A couple of things became clear to me through these meetings. Michael was smart, diligent, and committed to doing the right thing. He was introspective and tended to put others first and himself second or third.

I noticed something interesting. Generally, people drawn to investment banking have competitive personalities. With his easy manner, Michael didn't seem to be that way.

He agreed but suggested that he was competitive in a different sort of way. I then posed the question that was at the heart of the matter—was he pleased with his progress so far in the firm, and how did he think the firm was thinking about the same question?

He paused and smiled for a moment. I assumed he was wondering if he should be open with me or not at this point. For the next few minutes, he shared that he was worried and not sure of himself. In Manhattan in his prior job, he knew the rules: every day was a battle, and only the strongest survive. Though he did not love that style, it was a simple game to play.

He thought his transition was not going as well here in Charlotte because it seemed most things went unsaid or it was assumed that he knew what to do and how to do it without any explanation from the firm. He found himself questioning every decision he made, and he often felt that asking for help was far too risky. Toward the end of his story, he suggested that he was losing confidence and was worried about failing. With a baby on the way, he felt quite shaken by his situation. Michael's confidence was the problem—and building his confidence back up seemed the quickest way to get him where he needed to be. We had to find his prior source of confidence and see if we could leverage that now to get him back on track. Confidence can be elusive sometimes; it can come and go for all of us—but we all can find it again if we know where to look. I suggested that he would be fine and that all he had to do was "trust your swing." But first, we had to go find it.

Michael's Seven-Slice Results

I introduced Michael to the Seven-Slice Method. Being an introspective and thinking person, Michael took his time and thoughtfully answered the questions. He chose to share it with his wife, as well.

Michael came back and summarized his results this way:

> The Family, Professional, Personal, and Physical Slices was where he spent 100 percent of his time and energy.

> The Intellectual, Emotional, and Spiritual Slices combined made up 0 percent of his time.

I asked him what he thought about his profile and if it provided a clue for him about what happened to his confidence and where it could be renewed. He noted that he probably had a different profile before he started working in Manhattan right after college. Growing up, his values were centered on family, friends, and hard work, but also included a strong emphasis on faith. In fact, his father was a retired minister and had raised him to have a strong faith in God. Whenever difficulties occurred in his life, Michael was taught to rely on his faith and persevere. Michael acknowledged that he had let the spiritual side of himself drift away in recent years. Although his spiritual life mattered to him, like anything else we ignore, it was no longer a source of strength for him.

The insight Michael had gained through his self-assessment was quite significant. While Heather was undergoing different challenges, she too felt as though she had drifted from her faith, which had once been important to her. The upcoming birth of their child galvanized them both to reinvest in their Spiritual Slice.

Together they joined and started to regularly attend a local church. To activate his Intellectual Slice, Michael began reading every few nights some faith-focused books that had been recommended to him.

Though he'd moved back to North Carolina two years ago, he confessed that he hadn't reconnected with anyone from his past other than his family. He had just been too busy to recultivate those relationships. To better attend his Emotional Slice, he messaged some of his friends from high school. They were happy to hear from him, and he soon began seeing them for a game of football or dinner every month. It became a treasured part of his schedule. He felt like he was now part of a community, and that went a long way toward boosting his emotional well-being.

None of Michael's choices were large or dramatic—but each gave him a sense of belonging he realized he had sorely needed outside of work and family. He began to feel calmer and more relaxed. This transferred into his performance and confidence at work. Over the course of a year, the partners' perception of Michael went from someone who lacked the necessary fire to succeed to seeing him now as a rising star with a solid future in the partnership.

Michael went on to do very well, and he and I have continued to work together in the firm from time to time. Though being a reserved person and not one for verbosity, he still speaks of the process he went through and is amazed how much it impacted him.

CHAPTER SUMMARY

You should take comfort in the fact that most people who seek a spiritual life do so because they feel drawn to it. If you're hesitating and wondering what to do first in your Spiritual Slice, just start anywhere. It could be going to a church, meditating, reading a few books on spirituality—it doesn't matter; just start. Once you begin to explore your spirituality, it leads you, not the other way around. As human beings, we seem to be drawn to spirituality by our very natures, but like anything else, you must start. If you're feeling a little stressed today as you're reading this book, it might be a good time begin.

ENSURING THE SEVEN SLICES DELIVER HARMONY

No person, no place, and no thing has any power over us,
for "we" are the only thinkers in our mind. When we create peace
and harmony and balance in our minds, we will find it in our lives.
—LOUISE L. HAY

Now that you have a good understanding of each Slice, how can you put the Seven-Slice Method to work for you? In Part III, we'll break down the process and share case studies to give you ideas and inspire you in your own Seven-Slice journey.

As discussed earlier in the book, there are many ways to become distracted when pursuing the Seven-Slice Method. So it's important for you to anticipate possible distractions and create a plan to ensure you can focus for short periods of time on each of these Slices. The process outlined in this section is remarkably simple. Commit some time and invest in the process, and you will surely find benefit in living in all Seven Slices of your life.

INTEGRATING
THE SEVEN SLICES

To make the most of the Seven-Slice approach, you should follow a disciplined process. As you've likely noticed from the stories at the end of each Slice chapter, the Seven-Slice Method boils down to three phases: assessment, reflection, and action. In practice the method needn't be so structured, but it's helpful to break down the process.

PHASE I: ASSESSMENT

This phase answers the central question, "What percentage of time do you spend in each Slice?"

Taking an honest inventory and figuring out what percentage of time you spend in each Slice of your life will illuminate any gaps or overages. Once you're armed with that information, you can tackle improving those percentages and work toward more frequent feelings of harmony.

Remember, your percentages must add up to 100 percent. That's all the time you have. My clients and I often laugh together because so many of them end up with a total of 300 percent or something like that when they first try this exercise, saying things like, "Well, I spend 50 percent in my Family Slice, 50 percent in my Work Slice, 50 percent in the Physical." But you've only got 100 percent!

Figure 10.1 provides a visual aid to help you assess where you spend your time. While the process works very simply, you will need to do it a few times to accurately determine the reality of the way you live your life today.

For our purposes, we'll talk through this exercise using the pie chart; however, you could also use the spreadsheet in Figure 10.2 to list the percentages of time you spend in each Slice over any given time period. Some people like to use both the chart and the spreadsheet to record their answers, and others prefer one over the other. Whatever floats your boat.

Look at each Slice of your life on the pie chart or spreadsheet, and quickly jot down your best estimate of how much time you spend there.

The key to reaching an accurate assessment is being honest with yourself. In other words, your answers should not reflect what you "hope" or "want" your life to look like. The benefit here is to get an actual picture of what your life looks like right now. Seeing the pie gives you a visual understanding of the value proposition that living a whole life can bring to you and those around you. This process will likely take a few tries to accurately capture your percentages. My experience with this process has been mostly working with individuals one-on-one as well as with executive teams in con-

Preparation Tool: The Seven-Slice Pie

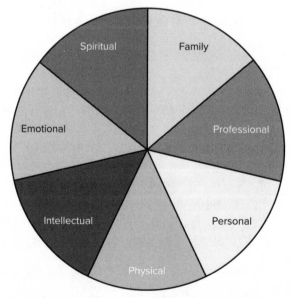

FIGURE 10.1 Assess How You Spend Your Time (Option 1)

Preparation Tool: The Seven-Slice Spreadsheet

Seven Slices	Self
Family	
Professional	
Personal	
Physical	
Intellectual	
Emotional	
Spiritual	

FIGURE 10.2 Assess How You Spend Your Time (Option 2)

ference rooms. In both cases, I've found it takes people about three attempts to get the accurate percentages. The reason for that is we all seem to have a mental picture of our time management system that may, in fact, differ from reality.

One of the challenges in this self-assessment process is that many of us look at this and attach our life-value system to the Slices of the pie. Meaning, say, if you value your family first, then when you look at the pie, you put this Slice as the highest percentage Slice in your life. However, upon further review, if you have a full-time job outside of the home, then that percentage could not possibly be realistic.

In fact, once this reality starts to come into view for a person, the reaction is often laughter: "What was I thinking when I put down 70 percent for the Family Slice?"

None of us want to gleefully admit that the highest value we hold dear in life shows up in a much lower percentage than we would have ever thought much about.

It's critical to work through this exercise with a judgment-free mindset. The point isn't to make yourself feel bad about where your time was spent prior to undertaking this process. Feeling bad about your circumstances won't change them. The point is to use these percentages as a jumping-off point to help you manage your stress and, if necessary, to intervene in Slices where you want to increase or decrease your time.

PHASE II: REFLECTION

Now that you've got an accurate sense of how you spend your time, how do you feel about your results? Were there any Slice percentages that surprised you? Were there any that pleased or disappointed you?

Go through each Slice and answer the following questions. These questions aren't meant to judge you. Rather, they can help guide you to a practical way to touch each of your Slices and find a way to achieve greater harmony and a sense of balance. The purpose is to find insights into why you spend a fair amount of time in some Slices and little to no time in other Slices.

The Family Slice

1. Per week, what percentage of my time do I spend in my family life?

2. When I am there, how available am I?

3. If I could, would I spend more time there?

The Professional Slice

1. Per week, what percentage of time does this take for me?

2. Does it creep into other Slices when I am spending time in those?

3. Am I in control, or is my work in control of the time?

The Personal Slice

1. Per week, what percentage of my time do I spend on something I choose to do just for myself?

2. If I do not spend time here now, when did I last remember spending some time here?

3. Is there an apparent reason why I don't?

The Physical Slice

1. Per week, what percentage of my time do I spend exercising and taking care of myself either formally or informally?

2. If I do exercise, do I schedule it, or is it random and based on convenience?

3. If I don't exercise, why don't I?

The Intellectual Slice

1. Per week, how much time do I spend reading or pursuing an intellectual interest?

2. If I don't, did I at some point in my life? If so, why did I stop?

3. If I never have spent time here, what am I curious enough about to want to start now?

The Emotional Slice

1. Per week, how often (or if at all) do I spend thinking about my feelings?

2. Am I in control of them, or are they in control of me?

3. Would having a better understanding of my emotions benefit me in my overall life?

4. If yes, what would be a practical next step?

The Spiritual Slice

1. Per week, what percentage of my time is spent in my spiritual life?

2. If little to none today, was there a point in my life when I did, and why did I stop?

3. How would I start if I wanted to begin or renew this part of my life?

COMMON OBSERVATIONS AND REACTIONS

The first observation most people make is that some of their Slices have a zero or a single-digit number in the percentage column. It does not seem unusual at all to see two to three Slices with virtually no activity or time spent in them for years. For some people, this realization will be a surprise; for others, it will only be a confirmation of what they already suspected.

The second observation many people make is that they didn't *deliberately* drop the currently empty or thin Slices out of their lives. In many cases another Slice, or nothing, took their place in the person's life.

For instance, someone might not have intentionally stopped having a personal life, but work and family obligations made her too busy to maintain one. Or maybe someone stopped attending his book club during an exceptionally busy time and just never picked it back up.

When confronted with the fact that they've left parts of their life dormant, many people immediately respond, "Well, it would be great to do more in [my dormant Slice(s)], but I don't have any spare time for that."

That dismissive response is a very human reaction to the idea of change. "It's not as though I can add more minutes to the day," people tell themselves. This, of course, would suggest that the only way to increase the percentage in a dormant Slice is to take time away from a currently active Slice. That idea usually doesn't sit well as a reasonable solution. In Chapter 11, we'll share case studies where individuals struggled with time management—suffice it to say, it can be done. The path is to define for you the difference between being busy and being productive. What is simply worth doing versus what should be done well.

THE BENEFITS OF INCREASED SELF-AWARENESS

This process will have a direct positive impact on your self-awareness. Slowing down long enough to self-assess in a real and tangible way allows you to pay attention to you. This is not a selfish or self-centered kind of attention. This is almost like you taking a step back and just observing what people do and how they conduct themselves—only in this case, you are the subject.

This is a great time to follow your interest. So many times I have heard, "Oh, I used to love to do that!" when people realize that they used to love running in the woods when they were in college, or that they used to love gardening, or tinkering with electronics, or having dinner with friends, etc.

Our interests and our interest levels begin to come into view when we sit back and take stock. For some, it is a pivotal point where they see the need to change things dramatically. But for many, it becomes apparent that they don't need to upend their life to attend to their dormant Slices. Rather, just adding a few minutes per week in a couple of empty Slices will deliver a positive benefit.

In my work, I have observed that almost everyone over the age of 45 has at least two to three empty Slices in their life. Literally, they spend no time in 30 percent of their total life. It is not damning by any means; it is a statement of the times we live in where our time often feels "robbed," or it seems to be pulled from us by the demands of other Slices.

Awareness is the first step to regaining control over the dormancies in your life. When you do activate your dormant Slices, not only will you benefit by feeling more at peace and harmony with your life—you'll also be more available and able to help others.

You will also discover that you are unique. Really digging into why some Slices dominate your life, and why others don't, can reveal fascinating insights about you and provide the impetus for you to change aspects of your life.

STRATEGY AND ACTION

By now, I hope you've completed the pie chart and/or spreadsheet and quantified how much time you spend in each Slice. You probably have a good idea what's behind your results, and now you'd like to change some of those percentages. As you've read in the stories in Part Two, there's no "one right way" to integrate your Slices. Rather, the strategy by which you take your newfound self-awareness, follow your interests, and reconnect with all Seven Slices will be unique to you. In fact, it must be unique to you to be successful.

A note before you begin: When undertaking this work, it may be helpful to first identify your motivation style. Specifically, how do you do something well? Are you a self-starter? Are you someone who needs a partner or group participating in the same activity with you to stick with it? Are you someone who often starts off strong when beginning a new endeavor but will drift off if someone doesn't hold you accountable?

Maybe taking action means enlisting the help of your significant other, friend, or coworker. Or maybe you're more effective when you work on your own. In any case, knowing your style (and acting accordingly) can help better your chances of success when you undertake the Seven-Slice Method.

Addition, Not Subtraction

I like to suggest that the solution is by addition, not subtraction. Obviously, you want to spend *some* more time in the Slices of your life where you find yourself spending little to no time—but in many cases it's not practical (or a good idea) to take time away from other Slices, like work or family. Instead, try to find the remote or empty areas in your life and then fill them with activities that revolve around your dormant Slices. You probably won't equalize the percentages spent in each Slice this way, but you will feel a clear *sense* of being more balanced.

What is creating this sense of balance is the heightened awareness of living in harmony with all Seven Slices of your life.

SETTING BOUNDARIES

Learning how to set boundaries is a skill that many people find improves their ability to spend time in all their Slices. The process of focusing on and appreciating the Seven Slices of one's life has a way of getting people to finally set time aside for all of them. For many people, this process changes how they think about the value of their time.

The decision about where to spend your time is important if you are going to get control of yourself and your attitude as the busyness of life keeps charging toward you. You can't slow down life, but you can start to manage the cadence of your own life by thinking about and recording how many areas/Slices of your life you are engaging every week.

I think it is fair to say that most people have a difficult time saying no to requests, particularly when they come from friends, family, work colleagues, or members of their community.

Agreeing to too many requests comes with a price—by devoting so much time to others, you may lose a sense of balance in your life. You must be able to say when enough is enough. That starts with effectively managing time and setting boundaries.

I have found that boundary setting and time management get easier and less stressful when you keep your Seven Slices in the front of your mind. For example, if you need to spend more time in your Physical Slice and you are requested to coach your daughter's soccer team, the answer could well be yes.

However, if you are spending three nights a week running five miles and are already in great shape, maybe that request bears a further risk-reward consideration. It comes down to you being able to assess how to keep the responsibilities in your life in check or harmony with your entire life.

Think Micro, Think Tactical

Through the process of people deciding to spend time in their Personal Slices, they learn how to slow down, even for short periods of time.

This may seem simple, but I work with many people who run at such a fast pace that they need their adrenaline "on" most of the time just to keep up with the life they have built for themselves. So when they decide to pursue two Slices of their life (Intellectual and Personal) by scheduling a 15-minute reading time before they go to bed, that small window of time allows them to "turn off" their adrenaline and enjoy their reading and alone time.

Over a period, usually around three weeks, it becomes part of their habitual life, and the calm and the pleasure of the activity begin to take hold. The change in their attitude often amazes them.

When you make even a mild commitment to invest in dormant Slices and lead a more balanced life, your interest levels and energy will likely increase. Basically, when you take action to activate dormant Slices in the hope of living a more balanced life and you notice a minor improvement, it seems to release an energy and a sense of relief that you can control how you feel in the face of life's challenges.

Maybe you and your spouse have three children under four years of age, and you're wondering when you're going to officially lose your mind because it's become unbearable. Just spending a few minutes in one or more of your other Slices can be enough to give you a lifeline of hope and a reminder that this will not last forever—that your children will grow, they'll start sleeping regularly, and your life will calm down.

When your stress is all-consuming and there seems to be no way out, a sense of desperation often creeps in and builds slowly over time until one day it is overwhelming. When you counteract that debilitating experience by focusing on the fact that you have Seven Slices in your life, then the circumstances seem to become less overwhelming rather quickly.

Thinking in terms of the Seven Slices allows you to quickly assess what your needs are so that you can maturely pursue additional responsibilities without turning your world upside down because of them. As we all are aware, our society has been in a hurry for some time. A common complaint is, "How can I slow down and stop and smell the roses?"

Spending even a few minutes in the Slices that you were ignoring will aid you in finding that ability to "slow it down" long enough to create more mental ease and less dis-ease. I have found that it isn't necessarily the amount of time you spend in a Slice that matters, but the quality and the intention.

So think "micro": what small thing could you do to "touch" your dormant or thin Slices?

For instance, Rosa, a client of mine, found that she was spending no time in her spiritual life. At one time in her life, she regularly attended church service, but that had slipped away after she started working and got married.

Rosa wanted to spend more time in her Spiritual Slice, but it often felt like every minute of her life was accounted for. So she decided to start reading spiritual literature for a few minutes every Wednesday while she had her morning coffee. She enlisted the help of her spouse on those Wednesday mornings to keep her from dumping her coffee into a to-go mug and taking off for the office.

After managing to meet that commitment for the first month, Rosa told me that those 20 minutes a week were making a big difference. She felt it was helping to settle her racing thoughts that had been bothering her for some time. Once she started to experience the benefits of that time alone and enjoy her reading and thinking, she increased the frequency to a few times a week. For Rosa a small investment of time paid big dividends (and maybe it will for you too).

Like Rosa, once you identify and reconnect with a space in your life that needs to be filled, you very well may find an energy is released, and you will devote more time and take on more activities in that Slice.

A FINAL OBSERVATION

I've seen many people over the years start spending time in their empty Slices, and what I've found is that these people all seem to report an interesting observation: life feels more like a journey now, whereas before it felt like something they had to do or finish.

I think that observation has great merit. When you decide to "add" to your life, instead of "subtracting," by investing time in a Slice you ignored for a long time, the difference is immediate. This kind of self-care attention where you are learning or soothing or building strength creates an immediate positive feeling inside you. Having worked on this with people for years, I simply cannot see a negative to pursuing the Seven-Slice approach to find a sense of balance and harmony in life.

If you're a little overwhelmed, try answering the questions below to help get you started and navigate the process:

Assessment

- What percentage of time do you currently spend in each Slice?
- Can you validate your estimates?
- Where do you actually spend your time, if different?
- How present are you in each of your Slices?

Reflection

- Are your percentages where you'd like them to be?
- If not, why not? Drill down here and go beyond just, "I don't have time." Try to track the reason why each Slice percentage is what it is.

Strategy and Action

- What's in your power to change? What boundaries might you put in place to make sure you touch each of your Slices each week?
- Are there activities that interest you? What would be the lowest time commitment you would need to touch your dormant Slices? If your interests are in larger, more involved projects, how could you break them down so that they fit into your schedule?
- Are there activities you might integrate into your schedule that could contribute to two or more Slices?

What do you think? Time to give it a try?

In the next chapter we'll look at a few examples of how others have generated their own percentages and what they did with the information.

CASE STUDIES OF THE SEVEN-SLICE HARMONY

You've already learned from Part Two that no two people engage with the Seven-Slice Method the same way. In this chapter, we share three more case studies from my consulting work. Just like the stories shared in each Slice chapter, these are fictionalized accounts of clients I've worked with who utilized the Seven-Slice Method to gain a greater sense of calm and control amid their successful, busy lives.

These case studies are offered here to further inspire your own Seven-Slice journey.

CASE STUDY 1: JAMES

James was at a roadblock in his career in a generic pharmaceutical company. A friendly, gregarious person, James had been working in pharmaceutical sales for 15 years.

When James and I met, he had recently left the sales division after a rough period and had moved into a challenging new role in which he had little functional background. We were to work on the transition and build new executive skills that his new position would require, particularly leadership skills.

As we began our relationship, the full picture of his life came into view. His family life was cracking. For years James had been unhappy with his wife, and his three young children had picked up on the tension between their parents, bracing themselves whenever James and his wife raised their voices. That obviously weighed heavily on James and his wife.

James had gained about 20 pounds in the last year, which he believed contributed to his lack of energy. Constantly feeling like a bad husband, a bad father, and a bad exerciser reduced his self-confidence—which in turn negatively impacted his performance in his new position. He was managing himself at work well enough that no one was aware that he was struggling, but he was concerned that his mounting stress could soon become overwhelming.

Remember the Selye quote about stress? "It's not stress that kills us; it is our reaction to it." James was an astute person who had already achieved financial success. He was keenly aware that performance and confidence mattered in his business career. Like most of us, he dealt with many life challenges before—but in the past those challenges had typically been staggered, where one thing might go wrong here and there, but never had everything gone wrong all at once. For the first time in his life, it felt like everything was going wrong at the same time. This "everything-at-once" situation kept James worrying night and day, and his stress continued to worsen.

The feeling of being overwhelmed paralyzed James. It was time to break things down so that he could better manage his debilitating and ever-worsening stress. I offered two different suggestions to help him pinpoint what he could control and how to deal with the rest that was out of his control.

How Do You Prioritize in Overwhelm?

My first suggestion was to intervene in the everything-at-once feeling. I suspected that breaking things down into a priority order would help James immensely. I've used the following method for many years to help my clients find their way back from the feeling of being overwhelmed.

In many cases, when people are working as fast as they can—and then they need to move faster—I advise them to slow down. When you're on personal overwhelm, you need to sort the most critical and important things from the things you can delay until you have a better chance to address them. People who are addicted to responsibility—the folks who take on every project, every initiative, every task because they can—often reach overwhelm very quickly and panic. The best thing to do is stop and see what you need to do and what you *can* do. You can't do everything, but there are times when you cannot fail. This exercise better equips you to succeed.

First, I asked James to make a list of everything that was stressing him out—everything, large and small. We wrote them all down on a whiteboard.

Second, he needed to assign the gravity of each item and the urgency with which it needed to be addressed. For each stressor on his list, I asked him to give it one of the following labels:

- **Issue.** Anything that needs a solution tomorrow.
- **Problem.** Anything that needs a solution today.
- **Crisis.** Anything that needed a solution yesterday.
- **Catastrophe.** Anything that needs a Plan B.

I impressed on James that the key to this step was to be honest about when each issue *actually* needed attention and/or a solution, not when it *felt* like it did (when people are feeling overwhelmed, everything on their plate feels like it needs to be resolved that very day).

Third, we evaluated his results. As James began to review his situation, it became clear to him that focusing on problems before they had the chance to reach the crisis state was critical. Making sure to find the problems that had available solutions ("easy wins") was also priority number one.

His evaluation revealed that there were no pending catastrophes. Moreover, identifying the issues that did not require a solution *immediately* eased his worries, for sure. This three-step review process enabled James to get a handle on what he could start to control, which immediately reduced his nervousness, which in turn allowed him some time to exhale a bit. The feeling of being overwhelmed lessened.

Breaking Down James's Slices

My second suggestion was to look at the Seven-Slice Method to see where he was out of balance. Like most people, James had concluded that his work-life balance was the problem, and he was anxious about spending more time with his family in order to mend his marriage and keep his children protected while trying to learn and perform in his new job. It seemed daunting to him.

We started by understanding that the two major Slices of his life, Family and Professional, were taking most of his time and he had no more significant time to allot there—so achieving a mathematical "balance" was not realistic. After some debate, he agreed. I then explained each of the Slices to

James and gave him the assignment of measuring the percentage of time he was spending in all Seven Slices. I would return next week to discuss.

When we met a week later, he was a little deflated and asked in a rather flat tone of voice, "You really think this will make any difference?"

"It's the kind of thing where you'll get out of it what you put into it," I answered. "So it's up to you."

As I left his office, I wondered if he would commit to the process. For most people, part of the process is realizing that their stress levels and daily pressures have reached a point where they feel they must do something. Apparently, James was ready.

The next time we got together, his Seven-Slice percentage assignment had been completed. He seemed genuinely interested in sharing his results and mentioned that it was tough to get the percentages right, because in his mind, he thought he spent a lot of his time in his Family Slice. But after a couple of reviews, he came to grips with the reality that it was a much smaller percentage compared with the percentage for his Professional Slice, though still much higher than his other five Slices.

For James, that was an eye-opener. As he described it, he had a mental picture of his life and his priorities that did not match the Seven-Slice review. That gave him pause, and so we discussed it at length over the next couple of weeks.

He learned from his Seven-Slice review that three of his Slices were entirely empty, and one accounted for a small percentage of his time. As a person attuned to interpersonal skills and feelings, James could not believe he had allowed himself to drift so far from some of his core beliefs and values. He had all but abandoned his Emotional, Physical, and Spiritual Slices and was spending a limited amount of time in his Personal Slice.

This surprised and bothered him because he used to cultivate his emotional life by reading books on self-help subjects and attending conferences on motivating and inspiring executive teams. He had grown up a religious person who attended church regularly—but after his review he'd realized he had not set foot in a church in years and had not prayed for some time.

In addition, he thought of himself as a highly active tennis player, and yet, somehow, he had not hit a tennis ball in over five years! He seemed to be a little hard on himself, and I assured him that this type of profile is not that uncommon these days.

So with the awareness part of the exercise completed, James was able to view his life's energy and time commitments in an agnostic kind of way without feeling bad about it. In fact, it helped explain why he felt so stressed out and overwhelmed. He was spending most of his time in his two primary Slices, and the other Slices were not able to provide him the release and relief that comes from accessing them on a weekly basis. With that reality clear and defined, he moved on to the next step.

The immediate challenge was finding time to invest in the other three Slices and undertaking activities in those Slices that would provide value for him. Over the next three months, he made a few decisions and slowly started the movement from no percentage activity in those Slices to some activity in each of them.

First, he ordered a book about Emotional Intelligence so he could serve his Personal and Emotional Slices with effort and purpose. He then decided to read for 15 minutes each night before he went to bed and after the kids were tucked in. This became something that took hold. In addition, because he often traveled for work, he read more in hotel rooms at night. The increased reading time felt like a bonus to him.

In addition, he suggested to his wife that they seek marriage counseling. After they started regular sessions with a counselor, the level of hostility in their day-to-day interactions diminished. While they eventually agreed to separate, they both noticed how their more amicable behavior toward each other had a soothing effect on their children, which made their efforts well worth it.

Second, after some delays, he visited his local church for a Sunday service. He wasn't sure how it would go, given that he had stopped attending in the past because it felt like too much of an obligation. He discovered that because he was now attending with the purpose of reconnecting with his spiritual side, the feeling was better. He found the rituals, the message, and the music comforting, so he began to look forward to the experience rather than attending out of a sense of duty or responsibility. Since comfort had been hard to find at that time in his life, the respite was most welcome. He didn't end up becoming a regular attendee—but reconnecting to the church did lead him back into his prayer time. He only spent a few minutes praying a day; however, he benefited on several levels,

Third, James bought a new tennis racquet. As luck would have it, his employer had a gym facility that included an outdoor tennis court. Once a week, he played a couple of sets with a coworker, worked up a good sweat, and called it a day. His spirits were lifted, his body got moving again, and he lost a few pounds. Not a bad result, considering that when we started working together, he had no activity in his Physical Slice. Spending time there, he reported, gave him both a mental and physical lift.

The short-term benefits generated by the Seven-Slice Method were now noticeably clear to James. He commented that with his new set of disciplines and his weekly regimen, his perspective and ability to manage his stress and anxiety had become a much easier burden to bear—even though his circumstances were the same. He was both surprised and bemused that embracing the Seven-Slice Method delivered results right away.

James and I continued to work together for several years. After a year or so, when the biggest challenges in his family and professional life were resolved, his confidence and self-esteem returned to a much better place. He attributed much of that to "working through" the challenges to a reasonable conclusion, but also suggested that he was able to deal with the challenges with more calm and resolve because of the effort he had put into the dormant areas of his life.

I recently caught up to James. He had moved into a new position with a new company. As we talked, he reminded me about the work we had done during his "dark" period, and he tried to give me credit for helping him to get to a better place. I reminded him that all I did was point him in a direction, and he did all the rest himself. He is remarkably happy, at ease, and confident in his life now.

CASE STUDY 2: KAREN

Karen was a brilliant chief medical officer working for a large bioscience company on the East Coast. Prior to working for this large company, she was the head medical officer for a smaller company, but due to a merger, she was now reporting to the parent company's chief medical officer.

She had thought of leaving and taking a severance package but was convinced to stay for a couple of reasons. One, she was very smart and knew the technical side of the compounds in ongoing clinical trials better than anyone else. And, two, she would have the opportunity to advance in management in the newly combined company, which was a career goal for her and one she had not achieved.

She was well set financially, she was single, and she was living in the city and had a vacation home on the shore. The people in her family meant the world to her, and she often took care of them. She had had a difficult battle with cancer in the past, but with treatment and time she had overcome it and got her health back into good shape.

The parent company was a client of mine, so because of the merger, Karen and I would now work together. She had never worked with someone like me, but she was a willing participant and very curious about what we could do together. She enjoyed the process a great deal.

My main responsibility was to help facilitate the integration of the two companies with a focus on melding the two company cultures. That meant I worked with everyone on the new company's medical team in order build a one-team atmosphere. Karen was coming from a culture that was very science-focused and that valued business execution over any other priority. In that environment, Karen flourished and enjoyed great success. She received regular promotions and was recognized in her business community.

The parent company culture was quite different. Though in the same bioscience sector, people and communication in the parent company were the top priorities in its culture. The difference was, if you paid attention to the people and communicated regularly, then the execution would take care of itself. As we all know, two different cultures can either complement each other or, unless they are managed carefully, create conflict.

Once the integration was complete, I was asked to work with Karen, whose work continued to be stellar, but her interpersonal skills were causing tension within the department and company. As frequently happens when two teams merge, there were a couple of "dustups" between Karen and other executives who did not appreciate her direct style. She was regarded as being a bit too blunt, and my job was to address that style and help her to become more collaborative in her approach.

I remember the first couple of times we sat down to develop this more tactful, collaborative style. Although Karen was pleasant, she seemed tense and had "loud" nonverbal communication language. Briefly, two studies undertaken by Albert Mehrabian in 1967 show that, very generally, 93 percent of our communication is nonverbal. Of that 93 percent, 55 percent is our facial expression and body positioning, and 38 percent is our tone of voice.[1] Karen's body language sometimes spoke volumes.

When I explained that to Karen, her reaction was, "Oh . . . " In that moment, her self-awareness level kicked up a point or two.

Karen's body language and facial expressions always gave away exactly what she was thinking—even when she didn't say a word. For example, if she was displeased with a statement made during a meeting, she would tap her pen repeatedly or roll her eyes.

Other times, she slumped back in her chair (with enough force that everyone in the room heard the sound) when others disagreed with her point of view. While she didn't make such gestures in every meeting, she did it often enough that she was starting to erode the good reputation she had earned in the company due to her great expertise on the science side of the business.

I see these symptoms often on executive teams. Karen wasn't the type to suffer fools—regardless of whether they were her superiors or not. Furthermore, her direct reports occasionally complained about her abrupt communication style and her lack of interest in their personal development. Given the new company culture was people-focused, this was a noticeable problem and one we needed to correct. Karen eagerly embraced the fact that she needed to improve her skills. She hoped to continue advancing in the company and wasn't going to let her communication style hold her back.

As I like to do at times, I wondered with her why she thought she was consistently having problems with communication when she was keenly aware of the problem as soon as we identified it. She paused for a moment, as if trying to decide if she should say anything, before finally answering.

She explained that she had been under a tremendous amount of stress. Over the past several months, her father had taken ill, and his condition was worsening. Her niece had been hiding a substance abuse problem and was now in full-blown addiction. On top of everything else, Karen's cancer had recently resurfaced.

At work, the integration of the two companies had proved challenging for her, with new pressures and people to process. With her personal life in turmoil and her work life rife with new challenges, she realized she was over-reacting or underreacting to things each workday but couldn't seem to stop.

Her medical doctor explained to her that if her stress stayed at its current high levels, she could eventually suffer health consequences. For her upcoming bout of cancer treatments, she really needed to be in the best state of mind possible.

She voiced frustration that though her life *looked* great from the outside, her entire world revolved around a stressful job and serious family health matters. In truth, she was not enjoying a single part of her life, which left her feeling a bit bitter and very vulnerable.

We talked about how stress impacts our health, our work, and our relationships with the people in our lives. She readily agreed that stress was harmful, but also observed that she had no way of making the circumstances change quickly. "This is the way it is though," she said dejectedly. "Nothing on my plate is going to change anytime soon."

Karen's Seven-Slice Success

I proposed that she give the Seven-Slice Method a try (after all, it can be a particularly effective approach when a person's circumstances can't easily change). She agreed with a smile, as if to say, "Why not?"

I explained the method and the pie chart and spreadsheet exercises (see Chapter 10) representing the Seven Slices, or areas, of her life. Being execution-oriented, she was drawn to the spreadsheet as a tool to break down where her time was being spent in her life. I left her with the assignment of filling out her chart profile, and then we would reconvene and discuss the findings.

At our next meeting, Karen was clearly looking forward to taking me through her results. Like most people, she had to take several swings before the chart was truly accurate. One thing had surprised her and brought her up short. She learned that she had essentially given up on her Personal Slice.

After some reflection, she realized that it started years ago when the cancer first surfaced. Through grit and determination and great medical care, she had defeated cancer—but had ceded her active personal life along the way. Prior to developing cancer, she had vacationed with friends on winter getaway breaks, dated from time to time, and volunteered at a soup kitchen in the city. Once the cancer was behind her, however, she'd never reclaimed the activities that had once brought her joy.

In addition to her Personal Slice, two more Slices were currently empty: her Physical and Emotional Slices. However, those two were no surprise to her.

She felt a bit energized by this process—again, she was brilliant and execution-oriented, so this sort of intellectual challenge was right up her alley.

"What do you think would be a good couple of next steps?" I asked.

"Isn't that your job?" she asked.

I still find that one amusing! As we've discussed elsewhere in this book, my role is only to point people in a few directions. Ultimately, it was Karen's responsibility to commit to expanding her Slices. Though it would require her to add things to her busy life, the benefits would add much more.

Because of her ability to focus on information and process, I asked if an easy starting point to reignite her Personal Slice might be to reach back out to the friends that she used to vacation and dine with. She agreed that seemed like a good place to start—her friendships had once added a lot of fun and support in her life, and in this moment, she needed to feel both again. She figured she would jump into the other two Slices later.

At our next meeting, she was smiling, which was a positive step in the direction of improving her nonverbal communication. That was a good sign. It turned out she had reached out to her old gang of friends. They were very welcoming, and they all suggested that getting together would be a great idea. They had set a date to meet for dinner sometime in the near term, and Karen was pleased and felt much better.

I pursued this. She hadn't met with her friends for dinner yet, but she already reported feeling much better. Why?

"It's something to look forward to," she answered. Sadly, it had been a long time since something happy and positive had been on her horizon.

I confirmed with some of Karen's colleagues and discovered that, yes, her newfound positivity had rippled out to a more patient and less glaring attitude at work.

I pointed out that feeling better had already had an impact on her professional life—all because she'd spent maybe 20 minutes contacting her friends via a group message and setting up a catch-up dinner.

That was an encouraging realization. Time was Karen's enemy; her days were packed with work and family—but it didn't take a big investment of time for her to reap a positive result. The payoff made it worth her effort.

We then proceeded to address Karen's other two dormant Slices. Karen was steady, consistent, and methodical; she did not start and stop things that mattered to her. I mention this because we all need to know our strengths when we start new activities. The risk for most of us is getting all revved up to start, but then losing focus and letting the initiative drift away, leaving us with a sense of disappointment and discouragement.

Karen was self-aware enough to know that she did not want to stop anything she started—it was part of her personal life charter and value system. After careful consideration, she told me she decided how to reenter her Physical Slice. Though the building she worked in had a fitness center, she wasn't crazy about the idea of her workout plans being public knowledge. Instead, she decided to join a fitness center near her home and signed on for sessions with one of the in-house personal trainers. She started very slowly, with one 30-minute session with her trainer a month. Starting slowly and increasing the frequency was part of her plan—otherwise she was convinced she would be unable to meet a more aggressive schedule. Fast-forward a year later: Karen had a routine that included a once-a-week personal training session and a walk twice a week.

The biggest benefit, however, was the impact on her attitude and health. Her energy level visibly improved, and she was more interested in work and people and in having fun. Once she was in a better mental place, she took a more positive and helpful approach toward her direct reports. She expressed curiosity about their goals and brainstormed with them on how they could move forward in their careers.

Keep in mind, this took time to settle in, but sometimes delayed gratification is the glue that can keep us in a good place. Since this area of Karen's life became a routine, she did not stop to think about it. However, she now had two active Slices of her life, Personal and Physical, that were making terrific contributions to the rest of her life, and she was the recipient of the benefits.

Finally, she was able to think about her Emotional Slice, the one area that she had avoided most of her life. She wanted to start very slowly and purposefully in this Slice, so she asked what she could read first. I gave her a list of a few books that I had found to be written for people like Karen such as *The Road Less Traveled* and *Further Along the Road Less Traveled* by Scott Peck. She was open to those suggestions, and so the process began. Karen wasn't the type to skim and skip around while reading. She really wanted to absorb and think about the material.

Slowly, Karen began to spend a few minutes reading twice a week. At that pace, it can take a while to read a book, as we know. But the beauty about the self-help genre is that each chapter can pack a message, so slow and steady was fine for Karen and her purposes.

The Emotional Slice is where you become more deeply aware of what drives your behavior and where you take charge of your own personal development. Understanding why you do what you do is a powerful developmental tool in figuring out how to live a more productive and happier life. In the next few months, Karen started to ask a few questions about topics that she found interesting in her reading. It marked the beginning of a self-reflection process where the subjects she was reading about created a framework for her to think about her own life.

Over time, Karen started to figure out why her reactions to people and the emotions she displayed in her Professional Slice produced some of the negative feedback she had received prior to beginning this process. Her emotions began to make sense to her, and that became the key in learning to relax rather than judge herself too harshly when disagreements with others occurred. The incidences of dustups, like the ones I had brought up to help Karen address, had been greatly reduced in number and intensity over the past year, although occasionally, there was an issue.

After she accepted that emotions are real and we all have them, she began to learn how to forgive herself and understand that to err is human, if you will. More importantly, she awakened to the feelings others have in the same circumstances. She started to understand, as we joked about at the time, that most people don't wake up in the morning thinking, "How am I going to annoy Karen today?" She began to realize that we're all juggling many things every day, and most of us just don't have the time or inclination to plot someone's demise in a professional setting.

Over time, her reading stayed constant, which worked well for Karen and how she liked to live her life. This newfound appreciation for reading and feeling more harmonious came to her rescue while undergoing her cancer treatments. This Slice helped her to process her fear and anxiety in a way that didn't lead her to anger and resentment, as it often does to people in those situations.

The gift she received—which is the gift we all receive from our Emotional Slice investment—was gratitude. Though she had been dealt a challenging blow with the return of the cancer, she was grateful that she was in a position to battle it without any other problems at that point in her life. The other Slices of her life were in fairly good shape, so she could call on them to help her along with her medical team to reach a positive and healthy outcome.

Fortunately, the cancer was defeated, her father recovered, and her life returned to normal after about a year, which added to her sense of gratitude. She continued to live with energy and purpose. Awesome.

CASE STUDY 3: ASIM

Asim was a very committed guy and determined to live his life in a certain way that included specific goals and timelines.

He was brought in to be president of a prestigious and successful executive search firm that I had been consulting with for the past year. The founder of the executive search firm and its CEO at that time was a unique talent, but he had challenges in managing operations and driving profitability.

His decision, which the board of directors approved, was to bring in Asim, who had served as president in his two prior roles and had stellar recommendations. In addition, the firm wanted to issue an IPO within one year, and Asim had successfully participated in an IPO in one of his former jobs in finance.

The recruiting process had been a bit arduous due to Asim's having to relocate from Manhattan to Chicago. This was challenging since Asim enjoyed living in New York City with his wife and two children (aged 8 and 11) and they all had grown to love their home there and the private schools the children attended nearby.

An arrangement was made to allow Asim to commute from New York each week for a nine-month period, whereupon he would be expected to relocate permanently to Chicago. He agreed, and I was asked to participate in the onboarding process with Asim and bring him up to speed on the executive team and culture that made the firm unique in the industry.

Working with Asim was interesting and challenging for me at the same time. He was a man of contradictions. He was a very precise thinker, did not worry about the details, empowered members of his team quickly, and was a bit aloof—all at the same time. He could be both charming and reserved. He was comfortable with people if there was a purpose behind the interaction and could be disengaged if the interaction seemed random or without a plan.

He was from Pakistan and had family there and in the United States. He had been raised in the borough of Queens in New York City and attended New York University for both undergraduate and graduate school, where he earned an MBA. He was raised primarily by his mother and had lived with her and his older brother.

When he entered the workforce after graduate school, he was determined to work extremely hard for five years, take a year off, and then reenter the workforce and follow that regimen for all his career. Except for one stretch where he worked for seven years instead of the five, he had adhered to that schedule.

I had never heard of executives running their professional life in this way, and I found it fascinating. Asim explained that he worked extremely hard during those five years and needed the off year to decompress and recharge before getting back on the ride again. The challenge was in finding companies comfortable with a five-year commitment and that offered a sizable financial reward at the end of that five-year period (assuming he was successful during his term). A very precise and careful plan.

Given his career plan, it made sense for Asim to join the executive search firm in Chicago. The company was likely to go public within a year, and that would provide a healthy financial reward to him when it was time to leave in five years to relax and recharge. He was extremely hardworking, focused, and strategic. He had an ability to build credibility with senior executive teams, and he was well liked and respected among his peers and direct reports. After my work with Asim on the onboarding process was complete, we would not work together again for more than a year.

At that point, I received a call from the CEO requesting me to reengage with Asim. It turned out that there was some friction building between the two of them. On several levels, it made sense. You had two powerful people in the top two positions in the company. Both were very smart and decisive, liked being in control, and were competitive by nature.

The friction encompassed a number of issues, but the most pressing was that Asim hadn't embraced learning the details and finer points of the business—and when encouraged to do so, he dismissed the advice, claiming his role in the firm didn't require it.

The CEO on the other hand was the kind of leader who could do every job in the firm (and in some cases, maybe execute better than the persons in those jobs).

It's hard for some CEOs to let go. The idea that he could do Asim's job better than Asim is what I refer to as a "natural tension" on executive teams. It happens all the time but is difficult to manage. Usually, the problem stems from differences in priorities. I agreed to get involved and set up time to meet with Asim.

When Asim walked in, I almost didn't recognize him. A tall man, Asim had lost a considerable amount of weight since I'd last seen him, which gave him a gaunt look. His voice had become raspier.

It did not take long to figure out Asim was feeling stressed and was under a great deal of pressure one year into his new role. As we spoke, I saw that his hands shook occasionally, very mildly, but nevertheless noticeable.

He listened to me politely and answered my questions, but he seemed distracted and not particularly present in the conversation.

I let a moment of quiet sit in the room and then decided to put my notebook aside. "What's really going on here?" I asked. "Would you like to chat about that rather than the tension between you and the CEO?"

Asim opened up quickly at this invitation, and an hour later his circumstances became clear. Over the past year, every part of Asim's life had taken a hit of some sort or another.

First, the travel was taking its toll. He had not traveled a great deal in his career previously, and now he had to travel from New York City to Chicago every Monday morning and back every Friday night. He'd learned the hard way that the Chicago weather meant that his flight was anything but reliable. He would often arrive home at 11 p.m. on Friday night and turn around and get on the 6 a.m. flight Monday morning.

Even with video chats, phone calls, and texts, he still missed his wife and children dearly during the workweek, and the distance was straining his relationships with them. Further, Asim and his family had not moved to Chicago after his first nine months (which had been a condition upon accepting the job), and this was another area of tension between the CEO and Asim. But even if Asim's wife and children left their lives behind and joined him, Asim still had other family in New York. Asim's mother in Queens had developed a serious problem with diabetes, and his brother was shouldering most of that responsibility.

On top of the stresses that commuting was putting on his family life, the search firm's numbers had flattened recently, and Asim could not find the problem. Pressure was mounting from the board of directors; the board didn't want to delay the IPO, but with the current numbers, going public wasn't going to happen.

At his recent annual physical, his doctor discovered that Asim's blood pressure was far too high and that he had lost an unhealthy amount of weight in a short period of time. His wife was concerned about him, which made him feel worse.

For the first time in his life, Asim had lost his naturally high sense of self-confidence. The direct and indirect reports on his team were bearing the brunt of much of the business pressure, and Asim was failing to protect them. They were starting to show signs of stress and fatigue. Two talented junior people had resigned, citing that the work pressure was not sustainable for them.

And one final note: he had just received a notice from the IRS that he was up for a random audit. A perfect storm.

We continued to meet over the next several weeks, and though there was some improvement in managing the tension level between him and the CEO, his overall wellness was not improving. His health wasn't getting worse, but it wasn't getting better either. He was on unfamiliar ground, to say the least. Prior to this moment in his life, Asim had run his career on his own terms and with great success. In his present state, all his ambitious thoughts and plans felt futile to him.

Though Asim was following our path toward rebuilding a better working relationship with the CEO, it was clear to me he was undertaking the work like an assignment rather than with a purpose. He displayed little energy or enthusiasm for mending fences.

One day during one of our meeting sessions, I decided to change the course of our engagement. He had told me he was a visual learner and preferred to see rather than just listen to the material that needed to be studied. I asked him if I could show him an idea that might be helpful for him, and would he mind if I illustrated it on his office whiteboard?

I grabbed a marker and drew the Seven-Slice pie chart on the whiteboard, labeled each Slice, and then sat down. I asked if he had ever seen anything like that before, and he just said no but did keep looking at the chart.

After a couple of minutes of silence, I said, "That's your life up there on that whiteboard."

He laughed hard at that one. "Is this what it's come down to?" he asked with a grin.

After my taking the time to walk him through the Seven Slices and explain the differences between them (and how some can be combined but none should be ignored), he started nodding in some level of agreement. I asked him if he might want to take the pie chart back to his hotel room and fill out the spreadsheet a couple of times. We could look at it together to get a handle on how to lower his stress levels. Being the kind of guy who goes after what he wants, he said, "I'll do it tonight and be ready to discuss tomorrow."

Asim Owns His Seven Slices

We met the next day, and he was quite interested in reviewing his results with me. He got up to the whiteboard and drew his chart and filled in the percentages in each Slice. Being someone used to being in charge, he wanted to own this process, and I thought it made total sense and it appeared to be working for him. He determined that he had three Slices that over the past year or more had all but disappeared from his mental radar screen.

His three missing Slices were his Spiritual, Personal, and Intellectual pieces. He understood missing the Spiritual and Personal, but he had previously prided himself on devouring all kinds of articles and books about business, politics, and sports, so seeing his Intellectual Slice being empty made him feel disappointed in himself.

As I have pointed out before, getting to the bottom of your Slices is not a judgment process—it's a process meant to give yourself an agnostic view of where you spend time in your life. Slices have a value proposition for each of us, and when we don't invest in them, we suffer the consequences.

Asim agreed, and then we thought about what could be done to start to turn on these Slices. By the way, I was convinced if his stress levels dropped just 10 percent, the tension with his relationships would drop by an even greater percentage.

His first step into the Intellectual Slice was the plane ride. Why not use that time to get back into the pursuit of the intellectual curiosity that he used to have? Over the past year, he had used the flight time to catch up on work and to rest and sleep. He committed to spending 20 minutes reading for pure intellectual stimulation, choosing to read for that kind of enjoyment rather than for duty or responsibility. So twice a week during his commute back and forth between Chicago and New York, he would have a Slice of his life to look forward to. That alone gave him a reason to smile.

He had married a woman from the United States who was raised in the Catholic faith, and she and their children attended the local church two to three times per month. Asim, being Muslim, did not attend with them except on major holidays and had let his faith drift over the years. It was nothing deliberate—just a casualty of a too-busy life living in Manhattan. He explained the Muslim faith for my benefit, and it seemed like he not only knew it well but had a spiritual connection to it. He decided to reenter his faith and looked forward to beginning that process.

His Personal Slice was complicated. With his current schedule, the like-lihood was that his travel, business, and family pressures were not going to diminish any time soon.

I have always suggested that many of the things you want in life can be attained if you decide to go get them instead of waiting for them to show up on their own. So I took a chance and made a suggestion. I pointed out that due to this challenging schedule, he had three nights a week by himself in Chicago where he usually worked late and then went to the hotel and called it a night. He mentioned that he had several friends from grad school who lived in the greater Chicago area. I wondered with him if it might be a good idea to have dinner once or maybe twice a month with one or more of them to just catch up and relax.

He chuckled. "Have you seen this movie before?" he asked.

"Maybe," I said.

Over the next several months, Asim and I continued to meet and work on the executive relationships in the firm. But at the end of each meeting, he reviewed his progress and his thoughts on the activities in the three Slices he had pledged to improve. Turns out he was solid as a rock in the Intellectual Slice, using the commute time to start the reading and engage again in his interest in business and politics. He found himself mildly looking forward to the chance to read on the plane. Reading passed the time faster, and nurturing his curiosity made him feel refreshed.

Over the course of a few months, he had only had the chance to get out for dinner with one of his friends from the Chicago area, but he indicated it was great to catch up and an enjoyable evening away from the business.

Though he and his friend wouldn't meet longer than it took to order and eat dinner, the social connection gave him an outlet to be himself outside of his work and family. "We've had dinner a few times," he reported. "It's been great; maybe we can reconnect again in the future."

I recommended he think about that a little bit. "If it gives you a brief outlet and escape and if you're doing something just for yourself and enjoying it . . . why stop?" I asked.

We went back and forth, and the net result was that over the next few months, Asim managed to go out once a month with a friend from Chicago. He was pleased, and it helped him feel more relaxed while on the road.

Although he had great intentions of returning to his Muslim faith, Asim had not made any great strides in that Slice during the time we worked together. However, he had started to reconnect with his prayer life. He was not praying five times a day (as the Muslim faith dictates), but he had started, and he found it provided him with a sense of rest and peace that he needed.

Over several months, things began to improve for Asim. He may not have been filling his three dormant Slices to the brim, if you will, but he did observe two things that made a difference. His level of awareness about his stress was more front and center each day. He realized that he had been close to being overwhelmed and at times felt like he was drowning from all the pressures coming his way. Knowing that he now had outlets to help relieve his stress calmed him down.

His stress had been so great, he had wondered whether he would survive the year, but now he was starting to see that all his problems had a beginning, middle, and end. For someone who lived with planning at the forefront of his life, this was comforting, as his plans were no longer his anchor. Rather than panicking that his best-made plans were being thwarted left and right, he gained perspective by living, just a little, in two more Slices of his life.

The Seven-Slice Method created a real difference in Asim's life by making him much more self-reflective. As he began to enjoy other parts of his life, he thought more about what his core life goals were. His comments to me began to go more in the direction of, "What do I want to really accomplish in life?" rather than to keep pursuing the five-year plan and rest program that had been his mainstay.

His reading and recognition that he had lost his personal and spiritual life hit him significantly. Even though he did not rush to fill those two Slices, he thought a great deal about why it happened. He gained more perspective, and he attained a level of humility that became part of his life. Until then, humility was not a meaningful part of his life or personality. He now believed he was on the path to becoming a better person.

That was probably more important than any other goal he could ever achieve. We continued to work together, and he became enamored with the Seven-Slice Method of reducing stress by activating all aspects of life. He introduced the method to several members of his own team, and he became a bit of a cheerleader for the approach, for which I thanked him profusely. It was refreshing to see an executive embrace a practical method to reduce stress and live more productively by utilizing all seven areas of his life.

I would like to report that he and the CEO lived happily ever after, but it did not go quite that way. The level of stress between them diminished, and Asim used his newfound humility to become closer to the details of his role. The CEO noticed the difference, and the two of them developed a better relationship.

However, Asim realized his family would never move to Chicago. There was too much in New York City for them to leave. His commute was no longer sustainable, and he was missing too much family time.

So Asim and the CEO (calmly and without tension) developed a mutually agreeable departure transition, and Asim found a good position in New York. The search firm ended up deciding to sell 49 percent of its business to a strategic partner later that year, and life went on successfully for both parties. Though the situation did not go as planned, both Asim and the firm made better decisions, and both flourished.

As a sidebar, while I lost track of Asim for a time after he left the search firm, I received an email from him two years later. He was in a business situation where he thought his team might benefit from the Seven-Slice Method. We reconnected, and the people on his team reported that they too got a lot out of the Seven-Slice Method.

The person Asim's story is based upon is the person who inspired me to write this book. Real-life Asim made an offhand but serious suggestion one day: "This method belongs in a book! You should seriously think about that!"

There you go, and thank you, Asim!

PARTING THOUGHTS

So what have we learned?

Several things, I hope. In reality, there really is no such thing as a "balanced" life. Most of us lead busy lives with a multitude of responsibilities and a wide range of distractions that make it impossible to maintain an even and balanced pace of activities. Moreover, there will always be days, weeks, months, or even years in your life when multiple issues all seem to come to a head.

By accessing each of your Seven Slices, however, you will be in a better position to handle the stress and more likely to reach a sense of harmony that "feels" like balance.

Harmony is an attainable goal. When you're regularly accessing each Slice of your life, then time is no longer the enemy. Even when your circumstances are dire and stressful, you will have the power to disperse that stress during the crisis point rather than having to endure it until the crisis passes. Having a consistent touchpoint in the five Slices that are outside of the Family and Professional Slices is the key to managing your stress during difficult periods. Every problem, challenge, or crisis in your life has a beginning, middle, and end. By managing your stress in a way that allows you to be your best self, you are more likely to achieve a successful resolution in any situation.

When confronted with a stress-producing crisis, most people take this approach: "I have to wait till the crisis ends before I can feel better." Sound familiar? That is one way to go, certainly. But the Seven-Slice Method provides an alternative that will enable you to find moments of rest and ease during the challenge and will give you a fuller and better sense of yourself along the way. Why wouldn't you want to give that a chance?

The least that could happen is maybe you pick up a new sport or a new hobby. The point is, there is virtually no downside to exploring the Seven-Slice Method. You may get to know yourself a little bit better, you may learn something new, you may reignite a former interest or discover a new one, you may meet new friends, your relationships might improve, you may feel better about your life, and you may discover a deeper purpose to everything you do.

Most importantly, you may begin to evolve and grow in positive ways. You may discover your own voice, your own passion, your own meaning in life. Perhaps by spending time in your other five Slices, you will find more meaning in your Professional and Family Slices, as well. This method can lead to a profound appreciation of how wonderfully complex our lives are, even while we're still just trying to get through the day and find happiness at the end of the road.

And remember, people around you will also benefit as you implement the method, because when you start to feel more relaxed and at ease, they will too. It's called the ripple effect, and it's a wonderful stone to throw in the pool of your life so others can enjoy the waves as they come to the shore.

Another lesson learned from this process, particularly when you share the process on a team or a small group, is that we are all the same and we are all different. Each of us does something different with our Seven Slices. We are totally free to spend time in each Slice and do what we want in it. There is no prescribed to-do list; there is no guru who tells you what to do. It's up to you. Something's lost and something's gained in living every day. Nothing is a waste of your time. As the Joni Mitchell song "Both Sides Now" communicates, we win something and lose something in living every day. Life seems to give and take something from us each day. Perhaps that's what makes life all worthwhile, and perhaps our purpose is wrapped up in there somewhere.

That being said, if you're short on ideas on how to activate your dormant Slices, all you have to do is ask for suggestions, and you will find people who will come to your aid. When groups participate in this method, I've observed that people encourage and help one another to find ways to live more fully in all their Slices. I believe the reason that happens is because when we are not competing with each other, we all want others to be happy and fulfilled. When people talk positively about how they are doing in a particular Slice of their life, the people around them always seem pleased and happy for the person. Getting that kind of support does wonders for people's attitude and builds better relationships.

Another benefit from the Seven-Slice Method is that boredom all but disappears. The five Slices outside of your Family and Professional provide a wealth of interest, activities, knowledge, and new experiences. From personal experience, I can assure you that there are years of things to do in each of those five Slices. There are so many wonderful books to read in each of the five Slices outside of the Family and Professional, that you may have to budget your time carefully to ensure you touch each Slice. It makes living life just more interesting. People have told me that spending time in these areas ignited a new spark in their lives and energized them to learn new things again. The important thing is to decide to begin to begin. It starts right there.

When a symphony orchestra is getting ready to perform, the musicians sit and wait for the conductor to take his place on stage and tap his music stand. All the players raise their instruments, and at the conductor's signal, off they go, performing as a unit. However, the musicians don't play at once as loud as they can. The conductor tells the whole orchestra when the violins need to take the lead, when the trumpets need to pause, when certain sections need to play together, all while keeping everyone in time.

If all the instruments are needed for the symphony to be successful, the conductor would never choose to omit a couple of instruments; otherwise the music would not have the same depth and texture.

I believe you are the conductor of your own orchestra. You have seven instruments to conduct, all seven brilliant parts of you waiting to play their part in your life's symphony. You choose their pace, their volume, and their frequency. You have the agency and power to bring about your own sense of harmony.

The hue and cry for more work-life balance is really a futile effort. It's the equivalent of expecting your work or your family to change to solve your problem. But it all lies within you once you understand and appreciate that you have five additional Slices in your life that can help you to create harmony and peace. I quoted Ralph Waldo Emerson in the Preface of this book: "Remember that nothing can give you peace but yourself." I couldn't agree more.

I truly believe that with the Seven-Slice Method you can find peace, no matter how busy you are.

I hope the message in this book provides you a path to move through your life with a bit more confidence, ease, and peace. There is always a way through the fog and darkness if we use our Seven-Slice Method as a guiding light.

The balance that you're looking for is not there because you, like everyone else, are constrained by time. But by seeking the harmony produced by the Seven-Slice Method, you will find a sense of ease and calm throughout the ebb and flow of your life.

NOTES

Chapter 1

1. "Work Life Balance," Mental Health America, updated 2020, https://www.mhanational.org/work-life-balance. Accessed August 28, 2020.
2. Ibid.
3. Katherine Torres, "Job Stress Doubles the Risk of Heart Trouble," *EHS Today*, October 9, 2007, https://www.ehstoday.com/health/article/21913936/job-stress-doubles-the-risk-of-heart-trouble. Accessed August 28, 2020. Ahmed Takawol et al., "Relation Between Resting Amygdalar Activity and Cardiovascular Events: Longitudinal and Cohort Study," *The Lancet*, 389(10071), 834–845, February 25, 2017, https://doi.org/10.1016/S0140-6736(16)31714-7. Accessed August 28, 2020.
4. "Stress Effects on the Body: Respiratory," American Psychological Association, November 2018, https://www.apa.org/helpcenter/stress/effects-respiratory#menu. Accessed August 31, 2020.
5. "Employee Burnout: Causes and Cures," Gallup, 2020, https://www.gallup.com/workplace/282659/employee-burnout-perspective-paper.aspx.
6. Harris Interactive, "Stress in the Workplace: Survey Summary," Lecture, American Psychological Association, March 2011, https://www.apa.org/news/press/releases/phwa-survey-summary.pdf. Accessed August 28, 2020.
7. Ibid.
8. Douglas Nemecek, "Loneliness and the Workplace: 2020 U.S. Report," Cigna, January 2020, https://www.cigna.com/static/www-cigna-com/docs/about-us/newsroom/studies-and-reports/combatting-loneliness/cigna-2020-loneliness-report.pdf. Accessed August 31, 2020.

Chapter 3

1. Adrianne Frech, "Healthy Behavior Trajectories Between Adolescence and Young Adulthood," *Advances in Life Course Research*, 17(2), 59–68, 2012, https://doi.org/10.1016/j.alcr.2012.01.003.
2. *Merriam-Webster Online Dictionary*, s.v. "trust," https://www.merriam-webster.com/dictionary/trust. Accessed August 28, 2020.
3. Erik Erikson, *Childhood and Society* (New York: W. W. Norton & Company, 1963), p. 247.
4. Steven Pinker, *The Language Instinct* (New York: William Morrow, 1994).

5. Betty Birner, "FAQ: Language Acquisition," Linguistic Society of America, updated 2020, https://www.linguisticsociety.org/resource/faq-how-do-we -learn-language#:~:text=Children%20acquire%20language%20through%20 interaction,is%20being%20used%20around%20them. Accessed August 31, 2020.
6. Atsushi Senju and Mark H. Johnson, "The Eye Contact Effect: Mechanisms and Development," *Trends in Cognitive Sciences*, 13(3), 127–134, 2009, https:// doi.org/10.1016/j.tics.2008.11.009.

Chapter 4

1. Phillippa Lally, Cornelia H. M. van Jaarsveld, Henry W. W. Potts, and Jane Wardle, "How Are Habits Formed: Modelling Habit Formation in the Real World," *European Journal of Social Psychology*, 40(6), 998–1009, July 16, 2009, https://doi.org/10.1002/ ejsp.674. Available online September 15, 2010.

Chapter 5

1. Matthew J. Zawadzki, Joshua M. Smyth, and Heather J. Costigan, "Real-Time Associations Between Engaging in Leisure and Daily Health and Well-Being," *Annals of Behavioral Medicine*, 49, 605–615, February 28, 2015, https://link.springer .com/article/10.1007/s12160-015-9694-3.
2. Daniel Goleman and Richard J. Davidson, "What Science Says About How Meditation Changes You Over Time," *Thrive Global*, September 6, 2017, https:// thriveglobal.com/stories/what-science-says-about-meditation/. Accessed 28 August 28, 2020.
3. Cherry Norton, "Left-Handers More 'Creative but Forgetful,'" *The Independent*, August 8, 2000, https://www.independent.co.uk/life-style/health-and-families/ health-news/left-handers-more-creative-but-forgetful-5370239.html. Accessed August 27, 2020.
4. Michael Corkery and David Yaffe-Bellamy, "'We Had to Do Something': Trying to Prevent Massive Food Waste," *New York Times*, May 2, 2020, https://www.nytimes .com/2020/05/02/business/coronavirus-food-waste-destroyed.htm. Accessed August 27, 2020.

Chapter 6

1. Elena Volpi, Reza Nazemi, and Satoshi Fujita, "Muscle Tissue Changes with Aging," *Current Opinion in Clinical Nutrition and Metabolic Care*, 7(4), 405–410, July 2004. Available in PMC, January 12, 2010, https://doi.org/10.1097/01.mco.0000134362 .76653.b2.
2. Mayo Clinic Staff, "Chronic Stress Puts Your Health at Risk," Mayo Clinic, March 19, 2019, https://www.mayoclinic.org/healthy-lifestyle/stress-management/in-depth/ stress/art-20046037.
3. Daniel Goleman and Tara Bennett-Goleman, "Relieving Stress: Mind over Muscle," *New York Times Magazine*, September 28, 1986, https://www.nytimes .com/1986/09/28/magazine/relieving-stress-mind-over-muscle.html. Accessed August 28, 2020.

4. Rainer H Straub, Firdaus S. Dhabar, Johannes W. J. Bijlsma, and Maurizio Cutolo, "How Psychological Stress via Hormones and Nerve Fibers May Exacerbate Rheumatoid Arthritis," *Arthritis and Rheumatism*, 52(1), 16–26. January 2005, https://pubmed
.ncbi.nlm.nih.gov/15641084/.

5. P. Lehrer, "Anger, Stress, Dysregulation Produces Wear and Tear on the Lung," *Thorax*, 61(10), 833–834, October 2006, https://doi.org/10.1136/thx.2006.057182. Accessed August 29, 2020.

6. "Common Triggers for Lupus." Lupus Foundation of America, medically reviewed July 18, 2013, https://www.lupus.org/resources/common-triggers-for-lupus#. Accessed August 28, 2020.

7. Judith A. Whitworth, Paula M. Williamson, George Mangos, and John J. Kelly, "Cardiovascular Consequences of Cortisol Excess," *Vascular Health Risk Management*, 1(4), 291–299, December 2005, https://doi.org/10.2147/vhrm.2005.1
.4.291. Accessed August 28, 2020.

8. "Stress Effects on the Body: Gastrointestinal System," American Psychological Association, November 2018, https://www.apa.org/helpcenter/stress/effects
-gastrointestinal. Accessed August 28, 2020.

9. K. E. Freedland et al., "Treatment of Depression After Coronary Artery Bypass Surgery: A Randomized Controlled Trial," *Archives of General Psychiatry*, 66(4), 387–396, 2009. Available in PMC, August 10, 2017, https://doi.org/10.1001/
archgenpsychiatry.2009.7. Accessed August 28, 2020.

10. "Your Lungs and Exercise," *Breathe* (Sheffield, England), 12(1), 97–100, March 2016, https://doi.org/10.1183/20734735.ELF121. Accessed August 28, 2020.

11. Justin Rhodes, "Why Do I Think Better After I Exercise?," *Scientific American*, July 1, 2013, https://www.scientificamerican.com/article/why-do-you-think-better-after
-walk-exercise/. Accessed August 31, 2020.

Chapter 7

1. Francesca Gino, "The Business Case for Curiosity," *Harvard Business Review* (September–October 2018), https://hbr.org/2018/09/curiosity. Accessed August 27, 2020,

2. Matthias J. Gruber, Bernard D. Gelman, and Charan Ranganath, "States of Curiosity Modulate Hippocampus-Dependent Learning via the Dopaminergic Circuit," *Neuron*, 84(2), 486–496, October 22, 2014, https://doi.org/10.1016/j.neuron.2014.08
.060.

3. Herrmann International, "HBDI Communication Styles Overview," PowerPoint, 2017.

4. Ibid.

Chapter 8

1. Jacob Morgan, "The Top 10 Factors for On-the-Job Employee Happiness," *Forbes*, December 15, 2014, https://www.forbes.com/sites/jacobmorgan/2014/12/15/
the-top-10-factors-for-on-the-job-employee-happiness/#7ae25fc45afa. Accessed August 31, 2020.

2. Roger Sperry, "Some Effects of Disconnecting the Cerebral Hemispheres," *Science*, 217, 1223–1226, September 24, 1982, http://people.uncw.edu/puente/sperry/ sperrypapers/80s-90s/224-1982.pdf.

3. Ibid.

4. Daniel Goleman, *Emotional Intelligence: Why It Can Matter More Than IQ* (New York: Bantam Books, 1995).

5. Athanasios S. Drigas and Chara Papoutsi, "A New Layered Model on Emotional Intelligence," *Behavioral Sciences*, 8(5), 45, May 2, 2018, https://doi.org/10.3390/ bs8050045.

6. Goleman, *Emotional Intelligence*.

Chapter 9

1. Michael Lipka and Claire Gecewicz, "More Americans Now Say They're Spiritual but Not Religious," Pew Research Center, September 6, 2017, https://www.pewresearch .org/fact-tank/2017/09/06/more-americans-now-say-theyre-spiritual-but-not -religious/. Accessed August 28, 2020.

2. Theresa Doyle-Nelson, "House Churches in the New Testament," *St. Anthony Messenger*, https://www.franciscanmedia.org/st-anthony-messenger/house -churches-in-the-newtestament/. Accessed August 28, 2020.

3. Nancy Colier, "Spiritual Beings on a Human Journey—Remembering Our Stardust," *Psychology Today*, July 6, 2015, https://www.psychologytoday.com/us/blog/ inviting-monkey-tea/201507/spiritual-beings-human-journey-remembering-our -stardust. Accessed August 28, 2020.

4. Dennis McCallum, "How to Motivate People," Xenos Christian Fellowship, https:// www.xenos.org/essays/how-motivate-people. Accessed August 28, 2020.

Chapter 11

1. Jeff Thompson, "Is Nonverbal Communication a Numbers Game?," *Psychology Today*, September 30, 2011, https://www.psychologytoday.com/us/blog/beyond -words/201109/is-nonverbal-communication-numbers-game. Accessed August 28, 2020.

INDEX

ABOUT THE AUTHOR

David J. McNeff is a thought leader, executive advisor, jury trial consultant, profiling expert, workshop facilitator, author, and keynote speaker.

A former collegiate athlete fascinated with peak performance, Dave founded Peak Consulting Group in 1995 to develop executive talent and bolster the performance of executive team dynamics for companies all over the world.

Peak Consulting Group focuses on behavioral management consulting, sales training, CEO mentoring, and management team building for midsize to large corporations. Dave has an unusually close relationship with his clients. Engagements typically last several years and include work as a CEO coach and trusted advisor, as well as executive leadership team talent development. In each case, the relationship includes senior-level executives and almost always an ongoing relationship with the CEO and/or the board of directors.

In addition to the advisory/coaching work, Dave also specializes in two other areas: corporate conflict resolution and litigation consulting. Conflict resolution work usually involves work in the M&A sector, and the litigation consulting is primarily focused on jury selection and legal team management, almost exclusively in the pharmaceutical and financial sectors. Dave is also a sought-after speaker for company and organization events. His style is engaging and very funny, which has led to many repeat events including hosting company annual meetings. Dave holds a BA from Providence College and an MEd from Boston University. Dave enjoys tennis and golf, and has three children who reside in San Francisco and Boston.